1 9 9 3

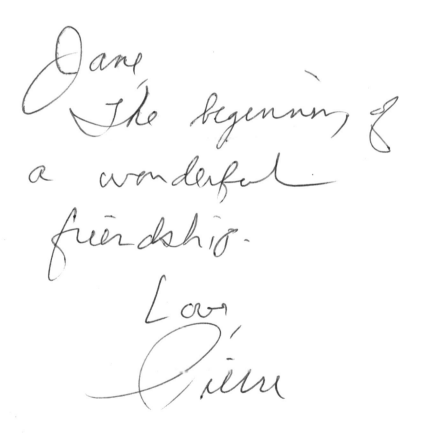

Jane
The beginning of
a wonderful
friendship.
Love
Pierre

Other Books by
Pierre Delattre

Tales of a Dalai Lama (Novel, 1971)

Walking on Air (Novel, 1980)

EPISODES

PIERRE DELATTRE

GRAYWOLF PRESS

Publication of this volume is made possible in part by a grant provided by the
Minnesota State Arts Board through an appropriation by the Minnesota State Leg-
islature, and by a grant from the National Endowment for the Arts. Substantial
additional support of Graywolf Press has been provided by the Northwest Area
Foundation, the Andrew W. Mellon Foundation, the Lila Wallace–Reader's
Digest Fund, and other generous contributions from foundations, corporations,
and individuals. Graywolf Press is a member agency of United Arts, Saint Paul. To
these organizations and individuals who make our work possible, we offer heartfelt
thanks.

Published by GRAYWOLF PRESS
2402 University Avenue, Suite 203, Saint Paul, Minnesota 55114
All rights reserved.
Printed in the United States of America.

9 8 7 6 5 4 3 2

Library of Congress Cataloging-in-Publication Data
Delattre, Pierre, 1930–
      Episodes / Pierre Delattre.
         p.   cm. – (A Graywolf memoir)
      ISBN 1-55597-180-6
      1. Delattre, Pierre, 1930–   – Biography.   2. Authors, American – 20th
   century – Biography.   3. Beat generation – Biography.
   I. Title.   II. Series.
   PS3554.E44Z467   1993
   813'.54 – dc20   92-39957
      [B]

Acknowledgments

I am grateful to the Bush Foundation for support of my writing. I also want to thank a few of the many friends whose moments of wonderment, so beautifully remembered, reminded me of similar moments written about here: Nancy, my wife; my dear children, Michele, Marc, Carla, and Jennifer; Alvaro and Barbara, Marcia and Marty, Bob and Marcia, Nina and Eric, Roland and Judy, Graham, Hendrie, Diane and Napoleon, Nor and Roger, the Leo and Dina group, the people of San Miguel de Allende, of the Northern New Mexico pueblos, of villages around the Española Valley, and my wonderful neighbors who gather on Monday nights at Marie's Café.

P.D.

for Alvaro Cardona-Hine

amigo/maestro

Contents

EPISODES

Prologue

Most of us tend to look back on our past less as a single unified story than as a series of episodes – moments of wonderment, discovery, epiphany that surface in no particular order, sometimes from some deep well of memory only once, at other times very often; but always when parallel events bring them to mind. The moments resonating most persistently are those that continue to perplex us until they illuminate our thoughts and actions, guiding us toward the happier and wiser turns in our lives.

I think we all need to keep a notebook or tape recorder around for times when such moments come to mind. It's the richest legacy we can leave for family and friends. People who know us would seldom guess which events matter to us most because these events are so seldom the ones that have given us reputation or notoriety, and often we alone experience them from a dramatic perspective.

One of the joys of writing is that it has brought me many friends. I tell stories like the ones in this book in hopes that others will share similar stories. Though I know that memory is inventive, I have tried to tell things as I remember them, editing out whatever seems like exaggeration until I was down to the bare bones of a single true paragraph. A few of these tales may seem pure fantasy; I can't help that. We all know that experiencing the miraculous can make us feel very lonely if we are forever keeping our mouths shut for fear of being thought a liar or a fool.

I wrote these stories down as they came to mind, then arranged them chronologically. Each stands on its own, so if you're a browse reader like me, you might enjoy just skipping around. I hope that you, who (like me most days) have time to read only in little snatches on the bus or plane, during work breaks, through the commercials, while waiting to doze off, will appreciate having a book that can be opened anywhere and read in short but finished episodes that are meant to provide resonance for continued amusement, thought, dream, gossip, celebration, love, speculation, and, above all, friendship.

– Pierre Delattre

The Ape
behind the Screen

When I was a little boy, I snuck into the attic while my father was away. I sat myself importantly in the swivel chair behind his rolltop desk. I opened a drawer and found a large book with photos of nude women in black and white. I studied each of the women. One had blond hair like my mother's; she was half lost in sunlight. The nude who fascinated me the most had wiry-looking pubic hair. She was a black woman with a beautiful sloping hip and pointed breasts. I was arousing myself, scrutinizing her, when I looked up and saw my father standing there. He said to me, "Never come up here without asking my permission." He pointed to a screen in the corner. "There's an ape hiding behind my screen. If you ever come up here again, he'll catch you and eat you." I didn't believe it, about the ape in the attic, so one day while Dad was away I snuck up there again. Just as my head got above the level of the floor, I saw the ape. He was orange, shaggy, long-armed. In later life, I would recognize him as an orangutan. He was swinging by his hands from one ceiling support to another. He didn't seem to notice me as he swung all the way across the ceiling and hung there as if staring at the wall. After I unfroze, I backed down the stairs fast and never went into the attic again. But the ape began appearing in my dreams. He would tap me on the shoulder and be standing there by my bed in the middle of the night. He'd tell me I had to go touch something or he would eat me. I got out of bed and obeyed. What I had to touch was always easy to get to – like the windowsill, the chest of drawers, the radiator. Once I'd touched what the ape told me to, he would make me promise never to tell anybody about him, then he would go away and I could with great relief climb into bed and sleep. When we moved to our new house, the assignments became more difficult. One night the ape told me to go outside and touch the tree in the front yard. When I was in the hall, I saw the light still on in my father's study, which was now downstairs. I tried to sneak past his open door, but Dad caught me. He demanded to know what I was up to. I took a chance and told him about the ape. He carried me outside in his robe and slippers, walking across the snow. He took me to the tree and said, "Touch it." I did. Back inside, Dad sat me on his lap. "The ape is gone," he said. "He'll never come into your room again." He didn't, though I found out a few nights later when my gramma sent me down to the basement for a jar of preserves that he was hiding in the coal bin now, ready to spring on me and have his revenge. Every time Gramma – who would not tolerate excuses – sent me down there, he would wait until I had the jar in hand, then spring. I always just barely made it up the stairs into the kitchen, slamming the door on him in the nick of time and smiling. I knew if anybody found out about him this time I was dead.

I Become a Lazy, No Good,
Worthless Dreamer

I'll admit it. I'm lazy. I'm no good. I'm worthless. I'm a dreamer. It's not my fault. I blame it on my father and my grandparents. My grandfather on my father's side was a famous evangelical healer in the south of France, pastor of twelve little churches. I can't remember ever walking beside him; I always had to run. His method of healing was in keeping with the work ethic. He in his long white beard and black suit would storm into a house straight to the bedside of the sick man. (I don't think he ever healed a woman, French women being so industrious.) His method sounded something like this: "But what is this! You're playing the sick one, *einh*? How dare you insult the Lord our Savior this way! There isn't time to be sick, *voyons*. There's work to be done! What would Jesus say if he saw you lying here like this? Rise! On your feet! Pick up your bed and walk!" Most often the man was so terrified that he would leap out of bed, while the women lifted their hands and declared it a miracle. Grandpapa Delattre was revered all over

France for these feats of religious terrorism. He passed the tradition on to my father, who woke me many a morning by bursting into my room at dawn, pulling the covers off me and shouting "What's this! You're still sleeping? On your feet, you lazy bum!" If I didn't leap out of bed immediately, he'd go fill a glass of water and throw it on my face. Mahma, my Finnish grandfather, was no better. After working hard all week on the farm making hay, we would drive to the co-op, passing – on the crest of a steep hill – the home of a man who was the leader of the pro-Russian Communist faction forever engaged in a polemical war with Mahma's anti-Russian Socialist clan. Alongside this enemy's house, the car always seemed to stall. While Mahma worked at the choke, we would see the man seated on his porch, leaning back in his chair, his feet up on either side of a typewriter, hands sometimes hovering over the keys but seldom touching them. My grandmother Mummu began the invariable litany: "That's Frrrrrrrred Thompson. He wrrrites for the *Daily Worrrrker.*" Then Mahma would growl, "Except he never worrrrrrks." They would turn to me there in the backseat, each with accusing eyes. Mummu would say: "Because he's laaaazy." And Mahma would add: "He's no goooood." And Mummu: "He's worrrrthlessss." And Mahma: "He's a drrrrreamer." Then, in perfect unison, just as the car lurched forward: "Heeeees a laaaaaaaaazy, no goooooood, worrrrrrrrthelessss drrrrrrreamer!" It wasn't just the normal rebellion of an American son against his French Huguenot tradition; it was also infatuation with the wonderfully musical expression of the lazy, no good, worthless dreamer concept as intoned with that Finnish burr of my grandparents on my mother's side. If they had just said the words in a normal way, I don't think I would have succumbed.

The Joy of Polio

I jumped out of bed on a morning of my seventh year and fell flat on my face. There was no feeling in my legs. I managed to pull myself onto the bed while screaming for my mother. She got me laid out on my back, then hurried to get my father. He ordered me to stand. I tried but once more fell. He put me in bed, propped me up on pillows, raised an eyebrow, asked a few questions. When he learned that I would miss final exams if I wasn't in school that day, he demanded to know what kind of game I was playing. Did I think it was this easy to get out of taking exams? "Stand on your feet!" I said I couldn't, I just couldn't. "He's faking," he told my mother, and walked out. Now I wept not only at what had happened to my legs, but at my father's disbelief. I'd always made straight A's, I argued. Why would I want to skip exams? She hurried downstairs. I heard an argument. Then my father was standing over my bed again. "Do you know what somebody has when they can't stand? Polio! Yes! If you can't walk, then you have polio. Infantile paralysis!

Shall we have the doctor come fit you with braces? Maybe put you in an iron lung? Or would you prefer to get up now and go to school?" He had to be off to work, he said, because life was no joking matter, and he better not find me in this bed when he came home. Understood? My mother took my temperature, saw with dismay that I had no fever. "Gramma's going to keep an eye on you. I have to go substitute teach. I can't play this game any longer. If you're still in this bed when I come home, I'm calling Dr. Bailess, do you hear? House calls cost money. Think of your embarrassment if he finds out you're perfectly fine. Think of the spanking your father's going to give you tonight." "I'm not faking!" I screamed with such anguish that my mother stepped back, stunned. I saw her struggle with doubt. "We'll see," she said. She left me. I tried several times during the day to get up, but my legs remained useless. I had polio, I told my grandmother. I knew I did. I finally convinced her. She phoned my mother at the school. Around five, Mom arrived with Dr. Bailess. He examined me, took her downstairs, murmured something. I heard her body thud to the floor. I listened eagerly. When she had recovered from her faint, I heard their slow climb up the stairs. They entered the room. He was helping her stand. He gave me a friendly smile. She looked at me imploringly through her red-rimmed eyes. He told me there was every reason to believe that I had only a mild case of polio. A few weeks in bed with my legs propped up on pillows, who knows, I could be walking again. "Really?" I said. "I have polio?" Oh, how happy I was. I had polio. I really did. I couldn't wait for Dad to get home. I'd show *him!**

---

* I want to thank my brother Roland for dragging me to my feet day after day and insisting that I try to walk. Without his persistent encouragement and faith that I could, I might not have recovered.

My Brief Experiment with Cross-Dressing

At age nine I was playing hide-and-seek with my older brother. He was looking for me somewhere up above in the first and second-floor rooms, but I had snuck past him into that scary place, the basement. I opened the wooden door to the clothes chute, backed my rump into it, bent forward, and sat on a pile of sheets. I tucked my head down and ducked back into the dim shaft. Then I raised up and, wiggling my way to a standing position inside, pulled the door closed with the toe of my shoe. I heard it click shut and found myself standing there in the dark. I panicked. What if it I couldn't get the door open? I kicked off one of my shoes and felt with my stockinged toe for a latch. There was none. If my brother didn't find me, I would have no recourse but to scream. The clothes chute went straight up to a little door in the back wall of my parents' bedroom. I knew they were up there taking a nap, so I wasn't worried about them hearing me, but the ape in the coal bin would hear me too; and I was anxious about what would happen to me when my father found out I had hidden in a strictly forbidden place, especially when he had made it clear so many times that I shouldn't interrupt his and my mom's naps for any reason whatsoever. I was looking into the pitch blackness above when the little door up there opened. Inside the shaft of light, through its dusty swirling particles, my mother had thrust her hand. She was dangling a pair of pink panties from the tips of her fingers. She said, "Oh, my, just look at how the little fellow's all grown up, ready to be a man." My father mumbled something. She released the panties. They fluttered downward; the door slammed; the light went out. The panties struck my forehead. They slid over my eyes, nose, and chin. I was smothered for a moment by an aroma of wilted roses. The panties dropped to my feet. I got my other shoe off and felt around with my stockinged feet until I was able to step into the leg holes of the panties. I scrunched down, caught hold of the elastic waistband, and pulled the panties up over my short pants. I was enjoying a thrilling but disturbing sensation when the door down there below my knees opened. My brother poked his head sideways into the chute, twisted it around until one eye was looking up. He was silent for a time. Then he grumbled, "You're it."

Schweitzer Claps His Hands
and Dances

After I read Albert Schweitzer's *Reverence for Life* at age seventeen, I made a show that summer of not stepping on ants. I suffered mosquitoes to drink my blood. Schweitzer's *The Quest of the Historical Jesus* inspired me even more, with a vision of the spiritual hero as one who is willing to throw himself on the wheel of history and bring it to a stop, even at the cost of his own life, so that we might cease our endless expectations of a future salvation and realize that we are living at this very moment in the fullness of time; the kingdom of heaven is in us now, not as a promise but as a fact. I practiced saying to myself, "Wake up, pay attention, you're in heaven," and found more and more often that I was. Thanks to Schweitzer's three-volume treatise on Bach, I was especially in heaven when I listened to Bach being performed at Rockefeller Chapel on the great Skinner organ. Knowing how I loved Schweitzer and Bach, the dean of the chapel asked me to serve as Schweitzer's French interpreter during his visit to the University of

Chicago. Like everyone else, I hoped he would play the organ for us. But this dear, hunched-over old man with his yellowing mustache, baggy black suit, high-top shoes, and string tie said his fingers were too rusty for concert making; he'd rather just spend a few hours alone at the organ. One night I walked him over to Rockefeller Chapel. While he waited in the dean's study, I went to turn on the lights at the board along an aisle of the nave. Word had somehow gotten around; an open door had been found. I discovered the pews filled with hundreds of people. I asked them to leave. They promised to be silent and begged to stay. I called the dean on a nearby phone. He said, "Don't worry about it. Schweitzer's half-blind and deaf, he'll never know." I exacted a promise of silence from the crowd; then, feeling horribly deceitful, led Schweitzer around the reredos to the organ. He patted the bench and bade me sit next to him. There were four consoles on this organ, which I'd heard Dupré, Biggs, and other virtuosi play with such diapason effect that the granite walls would shake. Peering through his pince-nez, Schweitzer pulled out only a few of the 103 stops. He played a passacaglia and fugue by Bach with utter simplicity, like the slow old man he was. As his gnarled fingers moved across the keys, I could imagine him shuffling along the paths of his jungle hospital in Lambaréné. He repeated certain passages over and over like a lover who can't get enough of them. When he was finished, he slid off the bench and walked into the chancel before I could stop him. He peered out, and was startled by a burst of applause. My heart sank. I thought he would be furious, but he cackled happily, clapped his hands; his eyes twinkled at the joke we'd played. In front of the cross, he danced a funny little jig until one of his shoelaces came untied.

A Little Stripping
Now and Then

The job required standing in a blast of 120-degree heat at the discharge end of a fifty-foot-long lacquering oven through which closely spaced sheets of tin, each stamped with twenty beer can labels, rattled along the conveyor rack at a speed that just gave us enough time to thrust a gloved hand at the edges, grab eight sheets at once between thumb and fingers, drag them out of the rack, and flip them onto a dolly beside us. Every twenty minutes, there would be a short empty space on the rack so that we could push one dolly away, pull up another, set blocks under the wheels, swill down a ladle of water with a big salt tablet, and, just in time, start tugging out the sheets again. I hadn't been working at this for more than an hour when I saw newly hired men up and down the line screaming for the foreman to shut off their conveyor before the sheets went flying over the edge and got somebody killed— they were quitting, this job was impossibly hard. By noon, only three of the eleven of us who had been hired that morning were still hanging in there. While we leaned against a wall, ate our lunch, and gulped down glass after glass of water, a slim little redhead in high heels and a short red dress walked past us, stopped as if surprised, asked cheerfully how we were doing, and told us that if we were having any trouble just come talk to her, she was right down there in the office at the far end of the factory. A few hours later, I heard the muscular guy with the tatoos, who was stripping the next oven down the line, scream for the foreman. His oven was shut off. He slumped to the floor. The foreman let him sit there for a time, then directed him to the end of the aisle. The tattooed guy returned with the redhead flouncing cheerfully beside him. She slipped on a pair of work gloves, ordered the oven turned back on, stepped up to the rack, and while merrily chatting with him began to pull the sheets out, flip them, and stack them as if they weighed nothing at all. The new employee watched with amazement until shame and male ego made him push her aside and get back to work. He never complained again. In a few months, the job was almost as easy for him as it was for her. Her name was Riva. She gave me the same treatment, and with the same results. I got to know her. She'd worked at Continental Can during the war when women had to do these jobs and the conveyor belt had been set at half the speed. Her boyfriend had been a military judo teacher. He'd taught her how to catch the machine's energy and go with it, just as you catch an attacker's energy so as to flip him easily with thumb and fingers. She said she was thinking of setting up an institute for industrial judo. Continental knew that most of the men stripping ovens stayed on only because of her, and the company paid her damn well to put on her little strip show now and then.

The Octopus,
My Savior

In the summer of my eighteenth year, I was doing volunteer construction work for a Presbyterian mission in Puerto Rico. One Sunday, I drove with Lois, the girl I would later marry, to the western end of the island, where we explored a beautiful crescent-shaped beach called Cabo Rojo. To our dismay, we were prevented from swimming by a horde of stinging jellyfish. We took a climb to a point that rose up at one end of the beach. From there we could stand at the edge of a cliff and look down on a clear pool with sparkling sands on the bottom. The pool was protected by a massive rock in front of it. The surf crashed against the rock, allowing the waves to wash around so that they swirled calmly and evenly into the pool. A needle of rock jutted out from the shore, just wide enough to walk out on and dive from. How tempting. This was a chance to show Lois what a brave and adventurous fellow I was. Despite her entreaties, I managed to claw and scramble my way down the cliff, bloodying my chest a bit, but finally there on my diving board,

15

looking up at her, the smug show-off about to do his stunt. I brought my arms back, crouched, and was ready to spring when a wave washed over my feet, bringing with it an octopus that immediately wrapped its tentacles around my ankles and held on tight. Though the octopus was not very big, I let out a shriek. It loosened its grip when the waters receded and slipped backward into the pool. Forget about diving in there! I clambered up to rejoin Lois. The little red menace was still swarming about exactly at the spot where I would have landed had I made the dive. In truth, the creature looked harmless now, and I realized that we could have easily shared the pool. I was angry that I had been made to appear such a coward in the eyes of the girl I was trying so hard to impress. Finding a big white stone lying in the grass, I picked it up, raised it over my head, and flung it at the octopus. The instant my rock hit the water, the octopus bunched up his arms and shot back into hiding. Then, zoom! – three huge shovelnose killer sharks charged in from either side of the breakwater-rock. They converged on my stone with amazing speed, thrashing furiously around it. I started to shake, imagining what they would have done to me. That night, back at the chapel during worship service, I was still imagining the scene of my slaughter. I envisioned the pool red with my blood. While the minister kept thanking Jesus for saving us, I was trying to assimilate into my belief system the new understanding I now had that we can never really know what appearance our divine savior will take. God had come to save me, not in the image of man but in that of an octopus. What was I to make of that? Later, from the American Indians, I would learn that the octopus was my totem, my ally. I have come to revere this many-armed creature, and to offer thanks to him or her on ceremonial occasions.

An Apple, an Orange,
a Pineapple, and a Banana

I shouldn't have bought the cup of sherbet from the little boy who held it up to my bus window in Querétaro, but it was my first trip to Mexico and I didn't know any better. By the time we were pulling alongside the curb at San Juan del Río for a ten-minute food stop, I knew I'd have to find a bathroom fast. I dashed from the bus into a restaurant. A waiter sent me running downstairs to a tiled room with a long row of toilets side by side. I hurried to the one farthest away from the open window, got my pants down none too soon, sat, and relieved myself profusely. Between spasms, I looked sideways and saw that a crowd had gathered on the downhill slope of the street around the corner. They were framed from head to foot in that large barred window, watching me with unabashed curiosity. One of the men yelled to someone to come see. The gringo was taking a shit. Perhaps they had never seen a gringo take a shit and they wanted to find out if he did it the same way as the Mexicans. Men, women, and children made cheerful comments to one another. To hell with it. I went on with my business. When I was through, I looked for toilet paper. There wasn't a clean scrap to be found. I glanced at my audience, imploringly I suppose. A smiling woman in an apron brought thumb and index-finger together a slight space and shouted, *"Momentito gringo, ya viene."* She talked to her son, a schoolboy in a blue suit and cap with a plastic schoolbag over his shoulder. He was gone. In a few moments, I heard his feet pattering down the stairs. He ran to me, stopped, pulled out a schoolbook, opened it, and tore out a page, which he handed me, his large eyes glowing with the pleasure of a mission accomplished. I said, *"Muchas gracias."* He said, *"Por nada, señor,"* and ran off. On the paper, with their names under them in Spanish, were an apple, an orange, a pine-apple, and a banana. I tore the paper into four pieces, used three, and left the banana on the floor for someone else. Quickly I pulled my pants up, zipped, and buckled. With a wave of thanks, I dashed up the steps and caught the bus just as it was leaving. All the way to Mexico City, I sat there marvelling at the unbounded spirit of Mexican hospitality.

Faking a Dream

Dean Hawley's vote was crucial as far as renewing my fellowship was concerned. But for some reason he never stopped to chat with me when we passed on campus, the way he did with other students. There was a student the dean adored, so I asked this guy, "Why doesn't Hawley like me?" He said, "Have you ever gone to him with your problems? Hawley doesn't feel comfortable until he has your problems in his bag." I said, "I don't see that I have any problems. At least not personal." The guy said, "As far as Hawley's concerned, that's exactly your problem. Go ask to have a talk with him. If you can't think of a problem, make one up. That's what most of us do." I said, "What kind of problem is he into?" "Right now he's into dream analysis. Feed him one of your dreams, man, and he'll be in heaven." "I can't remember my dreams." "So. Can't you make one up?" I called the dean's office. His secretary said he would be delighted to see me. When I got there, he rubbed his hands, sat me in the big leather armchair across from his desk, picked up the intercom, and told his secretary not to interrupt us for the next hour, no matter what. "Problems?" he said. I said, "Well, yes, if truth be told. It all came to a head with this very troubling dream." His eyes lit up. "Really! Tell." I made up a dream on the spot – one that I figured might get him to admire me just a little. I was sitting in this huge lecture hall, I told him. One of our most revered professors was discoursing on stage about Nygren's concepts of love. Suddenly this girl student leaps up shrieking, dashes down the aisle, throws herself onto the stage. She starts thrashing about, tearing at her hair and clothes. The professor claps his hands to his face and steps back in a panic. The students are all looking down at their notebooks. But I stand up. I walk to the stage. I gather the girl in my arms, carry her outside, sit her on the lawn and console her until she's calm and collected again. "What does it mean?" I entreated. Dean Hawley was silent for maybe ten minutes while he mulled it over. Then he said, "Freud's right, of course. We're never the person we appear to be in our dreams. In your dream, you're the hysterical girl and, because you were hoping that I could help you, I'm you. The problem, as I gather from your swagger on campus, is that you've been afraid to expose the feminine side – your true feelings, your hysteria about next year, your fear of dependency. Your intellect wants to smother the truth of your needs. You're afraid you'll lose control one day and make a complete fool of yourself." He pulled a folder from his drawer and wrote my name on it. "Let's start seeing each other for a little talk every two weeks or so. We'll work this out." I left feeling tricked and very bitter toward Hawley for stealing my glory, but I'd learned something: A fake dream is just as revealing as a real one.

Typecasting

Robert Elross was a genius at casting people for just the right roles. If good actors didn't show up for tryouts at his Town Hall Theatre in Berkeley, he would go out on the streets and find someone who acted just like the character he wanted to cast. He transformed real people into terrific impersonators of themselves. One of these — Howard Hesseman — went on to become the star of a television series by playing himself. As for Bill: he showed up to try out for *Death of a Salesman*. Bob listened to Bill read for Willy Loman, told him he was a much better salesman than Willy, too good for the part, and said he had a much better role for him: ticket seller. Bill was insulted. "Seriously," Bob said. "If you took on the role of promoter and ticket seller, there's no telling how far you could go. You've got the stuff. You could become a star." Bill wasn't amused; in fact, he found this rather insulting, so he left for Hollywood, where he thought his true talents would be appreciated. Three years later, he returned to San Francisco with second

21

thoughts about what Bob had suggested. He gave Bob and me a hand with promoting a theater we were running on Fourteenth Street, went on to booking shows for the Mime Troupe, then started booking rock bands on the big stages of the Winterland, the Fillmore. He managed to keep huge crowds of happy hippies under control while they danced under the swirling light shows, threw tantrums with the performers on stage, sat stoned out listening to Hendrix, Joplin, Jefferson Airplane, the Rolling Stones, B. B. King, all the best of them. Bill Graham became the most successful promoter of rock music in the country, a very wealthy, well-cast human being, thanks to Robert Elross.

Look at Me*!*

The other students in the first grade class I was teaching French to were eager and excitable. They would sit up straight and wave their hands, hoping I'd call on them. Not Jamie. He always sat slouched over, chin on his chest, belly bulging. While the others created vivid paintings, Jamie put nothing but muddy and shapeless blobs on the paper. No matter how many colors you gave him, they always combined into gray. I didn't even think he'd want to go with the other kids to the beach, but he did. I had promised that when they could give the French names for every object they might find on the beach or in the tide pools I would take them on an outing to Bolinas Bay so that we could make a collection for a school sea life exhibit. When they were ready – all except Jamie, who didn't seem to have learned a single word of French – we took the bus to the beach; the kids scattered out with their paper bags. The game was to fill their bags with objects that they would then show me, naming each one in French. While I sat on a dune, one kid after another ran up to me shouting, *"Monsieur, mon-sieur, regardez!"* and cried out the French word for the object found: abalone or crab shell, seaweed, rock, sand dollar – all beautiful, bright objects that shone in the sun. Jamie, who had shuffled off down the beach by himself and was standing hunched over glumly staring at a tide pool, was the only one who hadn't returned with anything to name. But just as the other kids were sitting down around me to eat their lunch, we saw him come lumbering toward us as fast as he could, holding his bag up, waving it frantically. *"Monsieur!"* he shouted, *"Regardez! Regardez!"* He stopped in front of us and opened the bag triumphantly. We gathered around to see what he'd found. In the bag was a shapeless gray blob. "The mud! *La Boue!*" he shrieked, delirious with the joy of it. *"Regardez moi! C'est la boue! C'est la boue!"*

Dumping on My Dog

My father was a joy giver: entertaining, creatively inspiring for everyone, including me, who knew him outside of our home. At home he was a tyrant who threw daily tantrums characterized by a bullying rage. When I was a boy he would make me pull down my pants and would spank me over his knee, hard with the flat of his hand. I sensed early on that he wasn't spanking me for anything I had done, but for his frustration at having to return home to a woman he didn't love "for the sake of his boys" (as people told us later, expecting us to appreciate this). He would drop my mother, my brother, and me off on my mother's parents' farm in mid-June, then be off to the Language School where for several decades he had a marvelous time all summer teaching, flirting, carrying on affairs (he pretended he was single), conducting his adoring group of madrigal singers. During his infrequent visits to the farm, he was especially wrathful. One time he took me over his knee and beat me until his hand hurt so badly he had to stop. Knowing that this had nothing to do with anything I'd done helped me to forgive him. The worst part of it, I realized later, was that I got the subliminal message: fun, especially with women, is to be had in secret, away from home. The real pleasures are found when one plays the bad boy, turns the wife into a mother, cheats on her, and then comes home contrite, but despising the wife, wanting revenge for her forgiveness. The spankings were also pounded into my unconscious. During my years in the ministry, I had a wonderful dog named Cindy. She would take long swims in the ocean with me, leaping into the waves and heading straight out to sea unless I called her back. She was so obedient that once when I told her to wait on a crowded corner of Chinatown, then forgot her when I came out of the store, I ran and found her still waiting there six hours later. I loved her dearly. But she kept running out in front of cars. Teaching her a life-saving lesson was my excuse for grabbing her once by the scruff of the neck from in front of a car that had skidded to a stop. I carried her down to the basement and beat the shit out of her with the flat of my hand. When this "lesson" was over and Cindy was cowering in a corner (she became a biter after that), I sat on the cement floor horrified with myself, wondering what in God's name had possessed me. Only years later, after frequent wondering about this shameful act, did it dawn on me that I was releasing what my father had pounded into me. I understood where child molesters, wife beaters, animal killers, and all the victims who go on to become victimizers come from. This is not to justify what I did to Cindy, but I have to say that I sometimes wonder in what even more horrifying way I might have "gotten it out of my system" if I hadn't done so by pounding it into hers.

A Sense of Humor

Once the two others guys in my gang found out my name wasn't de la Torre like the super had told them, but Delattre ("What? You're a frog?") they stopped being nice. "Look, Frenchy," Tony the foreman said, "We're stuck with you, so don't give us no trouble, just do your job, don't ask no questions and we won't tell you no lies." At midnight we'd go out with the switch engine, pick up a few boxcars at each factory's loading dock, then shove our long train down the line to the switching yards in South San Francisco. What I couldn't figure out was why Tony had me stand guard at the engine while the other switchman, along with the fireman (so-called in the union contract, though there were no fires to tend on diesel engines) walked into each factory and stayed there for such a long time. If I saw any cop cars or suspicious characters snooping around, I was supposed to wake the engineer from his naps so that he could sound his horn. I finally grocked on what Tony and his cronies were doing. They were running a bookie operation. The all-night pizza joint we stopped at every morning at dawn was the drop-off spot for all the money they'd collected. Just to show I wasn't stupid, I kind of hinted that I knew what was going on. After that, switching boxcars became perilous. Tony would have me climb up on the catwalk on rainy nights and walk to the front with my lantern. What with the train rumbling along fast under me, I almost fell off a few times. Tony had me stand facing the rear of the train, so I could see a signal he wanted to give. I chanced to glance over my shoulder just as we were about to pass through a tunnel that would have knocked my block off. I was almost decapitated again when he pulled the pin between two flatcars interlaced with lumber. The lumber went flying just over my head. While I was bent over coupling airhoses, he signaled the engineer to pull forward. The hoses exploded pebbles like gunshot all around my face. Miraculously, I was only grazed on the forehead. The super, a nice old cigar-smoking redneck, ambled over while I was helping gather up the lumber. "I should'na passed you off as Eye-talian," he said. "These guys got no sense of humor. Now they're trying to kill ya. I'm taking you off this gang and sending you over to work passenger trains." That was wonderful. I got to sit in the depot most of the night and read novels. One night I was crossing the tracks to where I'd parked my car when I came upon a pair of legs in boots and the bottom of overalls. I ran up the track to where I found the super. His torso was sitting there puffing on his cigar. He said, "Hey, kid, wanna hear something funny? I tried to jump from a gondola to a flatcar. Never let nobody talk you into a stunt like that. Not unless you want to get yourself killed." He pulled the railroad watch from his breast pocket, flipped it open, looked at the time. The cigar fell from his mouth. He keeled over.

The Swami Gets a Big Bang
out of the Bomb

Three bomb connections: 1) We're happy Boy Scouts singing away on the bus at the top of our lungs as we leave the mountains of Philmont Scout Camp on a summer morning, and cross the dusty flatland toward Cimarron, New Mexico. We've just finished another round of the chorus: "He raaaaaambled, he ramblod / he rambled all around, hey! / in and out of town, ho! / He raaaaaambled, he rambled / he rambled till they had to cut him down. / Billy the goat – bang!" The bus screeches to a stop. On the side of the highway in a cloud of dust stands an Indian boy holding a stack of newspapers under his arm. He's waving a copy, shouting, "Extra! Extra! Atom Bomb!" Our bus driver reads to us about the first successful explosion yesterday only a few hundred miles away. The news distracts us for a moment, then we're back to singing about Billy going from kitchen to butcher shop to bakery, to any place we can think of in town, busting things up, bang! 2) I'm somewhere in the High Sierras beside the John Muir trail, curled up in my sleeping bag next to Sam, my father-in-law. In the middle of the night, we both awaken to a muffled explosion. Were we just bounced off the ground? We sit up bewildered by a white light in which we momentarily see ourselves wide-eyed, with dry pine needles raining down around us. "Must be one of those atomic tests," Sam mutters, and we go back to sleep. After that I will become an antinuclear activist. While working for Stiles Hall, a peace organization in Berkeley, I will grow increasingly somber about the nuclear threat . . . until a moment, transmitted via public radio will break me free from the dead seriousness of my cause. 3) In that gloomy neo-English accent the announcers on KPFA have adopted, a panel of "deeply concerned experts" is introduced. They will be discussing the problem of nuclear testing. I hear the usual grave, academic voices deplore the dangers I am already too aware of. The only guest who hasn't spoken is the swami from India. Finally the announcer asks the swami a question in the form of a long statement: "Swami, considering the dangers of contaminated milk, deformed babies, cities made perhaps uninhabitable for thousands of years, groundwater . . . " On and on he goes detailing a worst case scenario. "Considering all these horrors, swami . . . could you give us your thoughts about the dangers of the bomb." Silence, and then we hear a chuckle followed by a burst of giggles, a guffaw, a voice so bubbling over with mirth that it can get only a few words out at a time: "Atomic bomb! Hee-hee, ha-ha . . . big bomb go boom! Blo-blo – Blow yourselves – ! Wheeee! Heeee! Blow yourselves up! Human race! Going-go-gone! Vani-Vani-Vanish! Wheee! Splendid! Oh marvelous! Goodbye-farewell. Oh-ho-ho-ho! Big bang!" There's no resisting it. Pretty soon I'm laughing too, laughing deliriously with the swami . . . until the program is cut off. Classical music comes on.

Ordination

I got a Bachelor of Divinity degree after three years' graduate study at the University of Chicago Divinity School, but I never intended to become an ordained minister. What interested me was the history of religion as it applied to literature from the ancients on down. I wanted to be a writer. But I got involved working with a youth group at the community church of Stinson Beach, and the next thing I knew they wanted to ordain me. I felt cynical about other ministers with their strained bonhomie, their forced pietism, the rounds of fat around their waists. When I was told to kneel down in the chancel of the stone chapel in Calistoga to receive the blessing of ordination from the thirty or forty ministers assembled there, I was feeling very little affection for them. I saw them as small men rendered ineffectual by their religious parochialism. I, haughtily, saw myself as Christian, yes, but also as Buddhist, Taoist, Hindu, and Hasidic Jew. For me, becoming a Presbyterian was just a convenience so that I could get the support I needed for my work with juvenile gangs. My eyes were closed. My knees were sore. A prayer was being intoned ad nauseum. I was wondering whether I'd be able to straighten out my legs by the time I was asked to stand – when I felt a rush of human beings behind me. I was rapidly enclosed within the body heat of all these men who had almost stormed the chancel. I could hear their heavy breathing as they crowded in. A hand settled on my head. Another hand. Another hand on top of those. Hands upon hands piled up, a great, heavy heap of hands shuddering there all over my skull and down my ears while voices said my name and blessed me. I felt a hot bolt of energy melt my brain to white light, then a warm glow through my whole body. It took me some time to gain comprehension, and to realize that these brothers were transmitting to me the blessing being sent through their hands by God. This was my first living revelation of what the incarnation of Word into flesh meant. It didn't make a true Presbyterian out of me, but it let me know in no uncertain terms that God was love and that God's love is a living force that is actually incorporated into the bodies of those who have opened themselves to receive it, and that they can pass it on no matter how theologically naive or provincial, no matter how indifferent or even scornful you may be of them or they of you. Their business is not claiming love for themselves. Their business is to serve as vessels and founts of God's love pouring into and out of them. My name henceforth would have new meaning for me. Whether I was called Pierre, Peter, Petros, Pietro, or Pedro, I knew wherever I lived that it meant "rock" and that I had been grounded by men inside the living rock of their faith. Later, when I became aware of the *chakras* in yoga, I would understand that I had received a transmission right down the main channel, the *shushumna,* from dome to foundation.

The Christt
of Stinson Beach

Members of the incredibly surly congregation at the Stinson Beach Community Church where I was having my first experience as a part-time minister had nothing but nasty things to advise me about their neighbors. Most of them weren't on speaking terms. They fell asleep while I preached, and made me sing the hymns solo. One morning a procession moved down the main drag, led by greasy-haired boys riding Harleys. Women and children were bunched up tight beside the drivers of six dilapidated pickup trucks stacked high with furniture. They turned up the street that led to the house of our church treasurer, Mr. Green. They had rented four houses on Green's block, each household headed by a master carpenter. They said they were tired of big construction jobs, determined to stick together taking on small, quality projects. We soon learned that the good life for them meant sitting in front of their houses at night playing guitars, singing, revving about on their motorcycles. Mr. Green was incensed. The last straw was when these people asked permission to use the social hall. There was no legal way of stopping them – yet – though nobody else had been social in the hall since it had been built three years ago. To have these hillbillies dancing and making music in there was an outrage, though you'd think the townspeople would have been pleased that the cabin-burning "delinquents," for whom I had failed to find more harmless social activities, were now spending their weekend nights quietly listening to the country music made by two sisters and their twelve-year-old brother Jimmy Larned. One morning the hillbilly carpenters saw Mr. Green working to build an addition to his house. They brought their tools, finished the job for him in short order. Ashamed for having signed a petition against them, Green asked what he could do to make amends. One of them said he'd sure like to borrow Green's hunting rifle. At home, the man pulled the trigger to show his wife the safety was on. It wasn't. The bullet went through the ceiling and killed Jimmy. The hillbillies didn't attend my memorial service, but three Sundays later they all appeared in church and shocked the regulars by amen-ing my sermons, shouting hallelujia, and singing the hymns full blast. So this was what Bible-thumping religion was all about. Liberal intellectual prig though I was, I loved it. Jimmy's sisters continued the same style of singing and hand clapping at the community hall. A town of dead souls came alive. At one of the packed dances, I stood marveling that so many of the folks merrily chatting or dancing had recently scolded me for refusing to announce from the pulpit that a petition was being circulated "on Christian principle" to have the carpenter families ejected from town on grounds of disorderly conduct. My congregation's resurrected sense of spiritual community had its source not in my preaching about Jesus on the cross, but in Jimmy's death on an upstairs floor.

Poems in My Shirt

I gave a speech criticizing the institutional Church as "the greatest impediment to spiritual life in America." Afterward, church people gathered around me to thank me for "really giving it to them." "We needed that," one of their leaders said, and asked where I thought the center of spiritual life was. "Out on the streets," I said, "among the musicians and poets." I discovered that church people like it when you make them feel bad about what they're doing – not because they intend to change their ways, but because they become convinced that they must be very good to feel so bad about it. I made the people at that Congregational church feel *very* bad. As a reward, they let me open up an experimental coffeehouse ministry on upper Grant Avenue in San Francisco. Working with Protestants, Catholics, Jews, and Buddhists I became a kind of nondenominational street priest. It was exhilarating at first. Young people in army surplus clothes and black leotards were practicing non-attachment, living in pads; the heated arguments of the old-style intellectuals rehashing history, ideology, and dogma were replaced by silent attention to immediate events that shape a more shamanistic identity. The existentialist/psychoanalytic preoccupation with "Who am I?" was replaced by fascination with "What is *that*?" Snyder, Watts, and the veterans of the Japanese War were discovering that Zen meditation with its sudden flashes of insight was more creatively satisfying than the traditional step-by-step analysis of the Aristotelians. Whitman became an inspiration again. Poets joined with jazz musicians; folk singers with street poets. Lefty laborers were meeting with artists and intellectuals in the coffee shops, bars, galleries, jazz cellars, and bookstores to celebrate a break from institutional life. Blacks and whites were learning what rich exchanges of sensibility they could share. But soon the sociologists were there to define the people in North Beach as "the beats," and then "the beatniks." Nonconformity gave way to utter uniformity of language and behavior. People who felt that life stops being fine when you define yourself or designate who your leaders and celebrities are were replaced by the self-advertising beatnik superstars. Despite my best efforts, I became one of them. When tour buses passed, the man at the megaphone would point me out in my sweatshirt and cross. I was another monkey in the zoo. Some of us retaliated by renting our own bus. Dressed in outrageous fashion, we toured about downtown commenting through our megaphone on the lives of the squares. Every day for me was some kind of far-out, too much, cool but groovy scene. My "mission" at best meant encouraging the growth of a loving community through nightly drumming, chanting, dancing, feasting. To collect poetry for our magazine, *Beatitude*, I had only to walk down the street and gather poems in my shirt.

The Fire
from Monty's Hand

The jazz pianist Monty Ross was initiated by his swami into a discipline that involved intense memory work. Monty quit his band and holed up in a San Francisco hotel to concentrate on his practice. He would sometimes walk into my coffeehouse in North Beach and immediately memorize long lists of numbers each of the many of us there would write down and tuck away. Hours later, after much conversation, we would get out our lists and he would recite our numbers without error. According to his swami, Monty explained, certain mistakes would be deadly. Breaking his celibate regimen, for example, would cost him his life. A red-haired beauty named Michael scoffed at this. She announced that she was going to seduce Monty just to show him that sex can't kill. Soon afterward, he shuffled in looking ghastly, saying Michael had triumphed over him and that he was going to die. His illness was diagnosed as leukemia with acute anemia. In an intensive care room of County Hospital, a group of us gathered to console him. Monty and the others were cackling away at the Yiddish yokes being told to him by a comedian crony. I cut in. I said this was no time for joking. Monty had some serious things that he should be thinking about. Embarrassed, the others left us alone. He took my hand, said, "Look, bubala, I'm on the other side of fear. But you're like a lot of ministers who visit the dying. You project your own fear onto us. I have other things to work on. I can't help you just yet. So please don't visit me anymore." Dismayed by the truth of what he'd said, I stayed away until a month later when he phoned and said cheerfully that he'd be dying at two that afternoon. Would I come read him from the Gita? Again I found myself holding his hand – this time seated on his bed at the far end of the terminal ward. A vein started to beat hard on his brow. "Keep reading," he said, "no matter what." He turned a greenish color, started to sweat. His eyes rolled back, his mouth fell open. A nurse hurried over, told me to quit reading. Though he was already giving off the death rattle, Monty raised up, waved frantically for me to go on. I did. She ran to get a doctor. Just after Monty stopped breathing, he squeezed my hand. I stood up in a panic. His hand was locked on mine. From it, I felt a hot electric surge flow up my arm, flower in my mind, charge my whole body with such an urge to laugh that I could hardly control myself. I looked out the window. The trees, grass, flowers, the people, the passing cars blazed with beauty unspeakable. I had a vision of the true glory of the world, followed by a mirthful rapture that lasted for days. Later, watching *Cinerama Holiday*, I saw Monty appear at the piano, enormous on the screen. He turned his head, looked directly at me, and laughed hilariously. I have wondered ever since what this gift he gave me was all about. It left me with a sense of spiritual responsibility beyond my ken.

Get Rid of Richard Night

I once knew a professor of chemistry who liked to parade his magnificent proboscis around the small college town I was raised in. He had won the world smelling championship by detecting blindfolded and without a single error 378 subtle scents wafted under his nose, but he would have been no rival for my friend, the poet Richard. From halfway across the city, it seemed that Richard's nose could pick up the scent of a friend's roast in the oven, a garlicky pasta sauce, or, even from across the Bay, a bouillabaisse, which was his favorite. His nose knew the subtle variations of each cooks' use of spices. His nostrils possessed a homing-in device that canceled out the work of unwelcoming cooks, knowing how to concentrate on those who would be too polite to turn away a visitor should he chance to drop by uninvited just as dinner was about to be put on the table. Whenever we served up an especially tempting repast to guests, we would say, "Well, it's about time for Richard to come knocking." Sure enough, the knock would be heard. Before one could decide whether to answer, the door would open and there he would be standing in his ragged overcoat, twitching his nose, knowing how to look at once pitifully hungry and deliriously appreciative of what he seemed so surprised to smell. He was a fine poet and a delightful raconteur, so why turn him away? Still, he had become a pest in the neighborhood, and someone finally had the nerve to tell him so. "Wonderful," he said, "then why don't you get rid of me? I have a brother in Chile, an anthropologist. He's invited me on a dig. I can't afford to go. It's in your interest to raise the money to send me. Think of all the food you'd save." This was at a time when a huge number of tourists were coming to North Beach. I knew we could pack in some three hundred downstairs in my coffeehouse. We posted large signs up and down Grant Avenue announcing that next Friday the public was invited to "Get Rid of Richard Night." On that night, Richard sat on a raised up platform looking just as obnoxious and disheveled as he possibly could—picking his nose, slobbering over his food, rubbing the edge of one foot furiously between the toes of the other. Ferlinghetti, Dienstag, Kaufman, Brautigan, and other local poets read diatribes describing various aspects—mostly invented, but sometimes true—of Richard's uncouth behavior. They begged the crowd to help us send him off to Chile. The hat was passed time and again. The more vile we made him appear, the more money was raised. He pocketed enough for airfare and took off. A year later, he sent us a postcard. He said the cooking in Santiago was fabulous, but he was getting homesick, and his brother was getting tired of him anyhow, so their friends were organizing another Get Rid of Richard Night. He hoped to be home soon.

I Can Just Imagine

There were two sweet girls in their mid-teens who used to come to my coffeehouse every day. They dressed in rotting leotards, gooped a lot of black mascara around their eyes like true beatniks, but they insisted they were saving their virginity for marriage; they never smoked dope or even drank wine. In the midst of the wildest North Beach orgies, they stuck together, remaining politely demure even though they were often the last to go home. I couldn't figure out why these girls kept seeking out a crowd with values so opposite their own. Then I heard a psychiatrist give a speech in which she said that when a parent repeatedly yells at a child or even beats that child for certain kinds of behavior, the child unconsciously picks up the message that the parent longs to behave in exactly the way that is being so violently objected to. The child feels compelled to carry out the parent's fantasies, even at the cost of being punished. Such a parent can often be heard to mutter to his or her child the clue words *I can just imagine.*

Shortly after I heard the psychiatrist speak, I happened to get a phone call from the mother of one of the two prudish beatnik girls. She said she and another woman, her best friend, were deeply troubled about their two daughters. Could I help? They could just imagine the kinds of things the girls were doing in North Beach. They'd been worrying themselves sick thinking of all that stuff they'd read about beatnik girls sleeping with those oversexed Negros, smoking marijuana, dancing with their clothes off for all anybody knew. I said, "I'm having a dance this Friday. Why don't you and your friend come. The girls are going to be helping with the cooking. You can just sit back, listen to some good music, put your worries to rest. You'll see. These beats are very nice people." "Well I don't know," she said. But she and her friend showed up for the dance, and before the night was over they were in a corner passing the wine bottle with a couple of spade cats, screeching their laughter, using words like *crazy, cool, groovy, too much* and *far out* and banging deliriously on bongo drums. They never left North Beach. They took to smoking dope, writing poems, wearing rotten leotards. They rented a pad just down the street from me and blew away their savings on some of the grooviest parties ever. They ranted on Blabber-mouth Night; took off their clothes and danced naked in the street; were proud when they got busted. They finally became a nuisance, pandering on Grant Avenue. I phoned one of their daughters. She and her friend had left the neighborhood the day after their mothers arrived. They'd moved out to the avenues, married very square men, and had children. I asked the girls if they couldn't come out, maybe talk some sense into their mothers. The girls gave it a try. But their mothers called them a couple of squares, told them to split.

The Ultimate Put-down

When Charles de Gaulle arrived in San Francisco for a banquet and formal address at the arena, I was invited by the wealthy Grace Warnecke to sit beside her at the head table and be prepared to serve as her translator should she be fortunate enough to engage de Gaulle in conversation. During the banquet, we found ourselves looking up at a long table where a very comical mixture of personages sat. Madame de Gaulle, Madame Couve de Murville, and other haughty grandes dames were dressed in empire-style dresses; they wore silvery headpieces piled high and glittering with jewels. Between them sat the frumpy, unadorned wives of our state and city politicians. As for the men, the snobbish French diplomats with all their looking-askance mannerisms sat in equal contrast next to the rough, untutored Americans, whose discomfort in having to wear tuxedos, whose inability to eat correctly or to make snobbish small-talk was making me feel great gusts of affection for them. At the center sat General de Gaulle, staring down his long nose at us with undisguised disdain. The mayor of San Francisco, George Christopher, was the first to offer a toast on behalf of the Americans. "Long live la General!" he cried. "Long live la Paree." Up and down the line, the French looked horrified. But Governor Pat Brown would make it even worse, for he would not only feminize the General, he would attempt to do so entirely in French. He stood, raised his glass: "Viva touse la mond di la grand nashonne di France. Viva la Madame General de Gall Aye je voodray especialité also dear, viva la General di la Madame di la General di Gall." De Gaulle's eyebrows ascended the Eiffel Tower of affront. He got to his feet, looking very tall and elegant next to the little interpreter who stood beside him. As he raised his glass and everyone stood and raised theirs, de Gaulle began to speak, his chin wagging with sincere emotion. "All my life," he proclaimed. "All my life," proclaimed the interpreter. "I have dreamed." ("I have dreamed.") "Of coming to this famous city. [The interpreter went on repeating.] This cosmopolitan city known throughout the world for its beauty, for the intelligence, for the sensitivity of its people. Here I am at last. What a rare moment. And so I lift this glass of your incomparable wine, and I say to you from the depths of my heart. Vive Chicago!" There was an appalled silence in the hall. Everyone held their glasses suspended in the air . . . until the interpreter, after opening his mouth, closing it and swallowing hard, recovered his aplomb and crowed, "Long live San Francisco!"

Saved by the Fear of
Posthumous Embarrassment

E rnest Dichter, the head of the Institute for Motivational Research, discovered that many people are afraid to fly for fear they'll make fools of themselves during an impending crash. He called this "the fear of posthumous embarrassment." He had the airlines build seats where you could feel less exposed to the sight of others. I myself was saved by the fear of posthumous embarrassment. I had been watching a crowd of body surfers ride the magnificent waves at the far end of the beach at Santa Cruz. Though a novice at body surfing, I waded into the water and swam out, anticipating the next big rise. As I saw it coming toward me, I stroked hard into it until I found myself being lifted incredibly high. Turning to ride the wave, I saw that nobody else was with me. All the others were way down there below, tiny people standing on the sand or in the shallows. In an instant, I could see that not a single other swimmer had been foolish enough to risk this wave. But it was too late. The skyscraper-high wave had seized me in its maw. It threw me out ahead of it, then lunged after me, roared, chewed me up, sucked me under, and spun me head over heels. I saw clearly, even as the swimming trunks were being ripped off my body, that I was going to be slammed onto the beach and killed. There was nothing I could do about that. But I didn't want to be seen lying there dead in the nude, surrounded by all those handsome young men and beautiful girls, me with my balls and pecker frozen tight with fear. Mortified by the thought of it, I caught my trunks with my ankles just in the nick of time, bent over with my head tucked between my knees, and managed while spinning head over heels to get hold of the trunks with my fingertips. I had just pulled the trunks snugly all the way up when I hit hard and found myself rolling onto the beach. A crowd rushed to see if I was all right. A lifeguard gave me a hand, pulled me to my feet. "That was the best executed roll I have ever seen," he said. "I want to congratulate you, man. Most guys would be dead after getting pounded by a wave like that. You're a real pro."

A Kiss of Death

Kimon Friar, the translator of Kazantzakis's *The Odyssey: A Modern Sequel*, took us out Greek dancing one night. I can't remember why I brought Schweitzer into the conversation but, when I did, Friar grew melancholy. He said one of the painful ironies was that Schweitzer had been the cause of Kazantzakis's death. Friar, who had lived with Kazantzakis in a cottage in the mountains, said the author was just like his character Zorba. He was always raving about wanting to hike down into town to pay a call on one of the women he adored. But this was perilous. Whenever Kazantzakis succumbed and got too near a woman again, he broke out in hives all over his body. After one amorous encounter, his skin became so inflamed that he almost died. He traveled all the way to China, where an acupuncturist cured him and then put him on an herbal medication, warning him that he was still very susceptible to infection and must stay away from places where disease would be prevalent. Passing through Europe on a reading tour, however, Kazantzakis could not resist visiting Schweitzer, who was back home in Alsace, in bed from a long bout with the flu. The two old men had corresponded for years but had never met. Overcome with emotion, Kazantzakis kissed Schweitzer full on the mouth. He caught Schweitzer's flu and died. From the author of *Reverence for Life* he received the kiss of death.

Noblesse Oblige

While having tea with Wallace Fowlie, the superb writer on contemporary French literature, I asked about his friend the artist Jean Cocteau. Had he been as charming as I'd heard? Fowlie said, "I'll give you an example of Cocteau's charm. He was living up in Lagnon, being taken care of by two rich old ladies who didn't give him much spending money. Nevertheless, he invited me to the most expensive restaurant on the Riviera. After we had been seated, he looked about, nodding pleasantly to the other diners. They recognized him, of course, and were delighted to return his smile. He summoned the headwaiter and said, 'Would you please tell that nice couple over there that Jean Cocteau and his friend would very much enjoy an aperitif before their repast, and perhaps a pâté as the hors d'oeuvre. And you might whisper to that gentleman at the corner table, say that Cocteau and his friend will be inclined to chasten their palates before the entrée with a crisp little endive salad, and of course your clear broth perfumed with those wonderful mushrooms from the Ardèche. And then, in due time, inform that pretty coquette who keeps making eyes at me that Cocteau and friend are inclined toward your incomparable duck à l'orange tonight. As for that distinguished family, it would be an insult not to succumb to their judgment as to a suitable wine. And perhaps, so they not be desolated, I should ask those good ladies to linger awhile should we decide later on to have a little bowl of raspberries in cream along with our coffee and cognac." Those who were asked were both honored and charmed to include Cocteau's needs on their bill. They were the envy of others who kept glancing at him, disappointed to have been left out, hoping for better luck next time." I said to Fowlie, "You were a friend of Wanda Landowska's too, I hear. Was she also a charmer?" He said, "Alas, yes, and a much more dangerous one than Cocteau. I used to own one of the finest harpsichords in the world, you know. It filled that space out there in the alcove. When she came to visit, she asked me to play something for her, then threw a fit. She said that nobody who played as badly as I did had a right to such a superb instrument. I must give it to her immediately. Up against a ferocious temperament like hers, what choice did I have? She was, after all, the greatest harpsichordist in the world. There was no point in even arguing about it. The next day, when four moving men appeared at my door, all I could do was stand aside while they took the legs off my precious heirloom, crated it, carried it out to their van, and drove away."

The Exorcist's Lament

I had been counseling a construction worker named Lenny. He possessed physical powers in abundance, but these only fueled his rage because he had not been able to channel his energy into building the psychic/intellectual powers he also longed to possess. For about three months, he came to my study for counseling, weeping, clenching his fists, pouring out his anguish and frustration. Then he started reading Ayn Rand. He discovered there were all these second-raters in the world; if you wanted to be a first-rater, you had to avoid them. He stopped talking to the guys on the job. He decided he was a first-rater who must hold himself in reserve for people of his kind. Despite my insistence that only second-raters so lacked humility as to think of themselves as first-raters, he took a trip to New York in hopes of revealing himself to the author of *Atlas Shrugged* as one qualified to join her coterie. A few nights after Lenny was gone, I began to wake up in the middle of the night with the most horrible sensation coursing through my nerves and veins – like some kind of poison, a burning, acidic torment of both mind and body. I couldn't figure it out because this was not my kind of suffering. I knew my suffering well. This sensation was absolutely unbearable, it was so alien to me. I didn't realize who it belonged to, but it cost me a week of misery, with sleepless nights of writhing in the bed. Then Lenny returned. He hadn't made contact with Ayn Rand, but he was jubilant. He said he felt like a new man. One night he had awakened with a start and found himself sitting up entirely released from his suffering. It was a miracle. I realized that I had somehow taken his anguish inside of me. How to release it? I went to an exorcist friend. She said that what I had gone through was common among certain poorly trained exorcists like herself who have a hard time releasing the demons they pull out of people. She said the demon stayed inside of her for months sometimes after the person she'd pulled it out of danced merrily away. "You're supposed to be able to fling the demon off," she said, "But I've never gotten the hang of it. I can't tell you the agony I go through." I said, "Can you exorcise Lenny from me?" "Are you kidding? From what you've said, no amount of money would induce me to take that man's demon inside myself. He'll be out of you in a month or so. I hope you can stand it that long. If you figure out how to get rid of him faster, for God's sake let me know." Lenny's demon was in me for six weeks, during which time Lenny went about radiating the kind of high spirits I knew belonged rightfully to me. The demon finally left me one night and returned to Lenny. I leaped out of bed jubilant. For months afterward, I welcomed even my most foul moods. I realized how precious our own familiar hell can be compared to the alien hell of others. Though Lenny pleaded, I refused to listen to his problems anymore.

Brautigan Done For

I never knew as great a fisherman as Richard Brautigan. One time we parked along a little stream. I opened the back of the station wagon and got to work preparing my gear. By the time I had finished selecting a fly and tying it on, Richard was already trudging back with his limit in the creel. He gave half to me and we waded upstream until we came to an encampment of picnickers. A mother and grandmother and three kids were splashing in the water. Brautigan bet me he could cast his fly right into the midst of those people and pull out a trout. He did, and so deftly they didn't even notice. Brautigan had another talent. He could get drunk on anything. In our tent that night, he got drunk on water. He began to lament about his trout fishing book. He just couldn't get the magic down on paper. He read me some of the stories and asked for a frank opinion. "Boring," I confessed. Then one afternoon back in North Beach we went into a hardware store so that he could buy some chicken wire for his bird cage. Suddenly he seized the pen from my pocket, the notebook from my shoulder bag, ran out and over to a park bench, and started to scribble a story about a man who finds a used trout stream in the back of a hardware store. The next day, we stopped to chat with a legless-armless man on a rollerboard who sold pencils. Brautigan called him "Trout Fishing in America Shorty," and wrote a story about him. From then on, trout fishing ceased to be a memory of the past, but the theme of immediate experience and Brautigan's book made him a rich and famous writer. He didn't handle this well and finally blew his brains out while working on a novel in his Bolinas cabin. I don't know what was bothering him, but here's a possible clue: The last time I saw him, we were walking past the middle room of his house. There was a table in there with a typewriter on it. "Quiet," he whispered, pushing me ahead of him into the kitchen. "My new novel's in there. I kind of stroll in occasionally, write a few quick paragraphs, and get out before the novel knows what I'm doing. If novels ever find out you're writing them, you're done for."

A Vow of Silence

Among the best poets of San Francisco's North Beach was Bob Kaufman, a wild, carousing, womanizing, raving and ranting but brilliant man who liked to antagonize the police by proclaiming on street corners, naked except for a pair of trousers that clung to the bottom of his ass, his "Abomunist Manifesto" for a world revolution of poets. Bob was half German Jew and half Martinique Negro. He had been a labor organizer, a gunrunner for the Likud. We all adored him and forgave him his drunken sprees. His head was shaped like a bowling ball, with enormous gleaming black eyes blasting away at you while he spouted full speed whatever free associations synapsed through his awesomely swift brain. As with some of the others, he finally burned his brain out on the amphetamine Methedrine. I ran into him on a street in New York where he and Norman Mailer, he kept screaming at me in triumph, were organizing the "beats" into a political movement that was going to take over the country. His mind was already racing close to the speed of light. I could tell that it was going to blow up and burn out very soon. He ended up in Bellevue Hospital that week. By the time somebody got him out and brought him back to North Beach, he no longer possessed the gift of speech. For the next ten years, mostly brain dead, he was unable to utter more than an occasional word. Shig at City Lights used to give him fifty cents a day so that, once he'd been taught to read the traffic signals, he could stagger over to Cassandra's for a bowl of soup. His wife, Eileen, took care of him and their son Parker, whom I had baptized. I wished that Parker could have known his father in his prime. I would find Bob in the park sitting against a tree. I tried to talk to him, but it was no use. Once he spoke my name; that was all. He was clearly not there, out of it in a way that seemed tragic to those of us who loved his former brilliance. The last time I saw him was in '68. Twenty years later, I returned to San Francisco. Bob was dead. There was a kind of shrine to him at City Lights. An authoritative book referred with awe to the ten years during which Bob had taken a vow of silence, as if the choice had been his. I read an article the other day by Herb Gold, again making a saint out of Bob, turning tragedy into spiritual farce by referring to that "ten-year vow." Whether it's a version Bob made up when he finally regained his speech, or whether it was made up for him, one wonders once again about the reversal process by which we turn the self-destruction of a generation's symbolic personality into spiritual victory in order to hype the cultural mystique. What other poets in history got so wasted that they weren't good for anything except being turned by their friends – out of what? compassion? denial? opportunism? – into saints?

Human Nature

he three of us got together before the confrontation on stage at the University of Vermont. Paul Goodman, our handsome crusader against commercialism, was pleased to find that I was an ally. Ernest Dichter, a plump, unattractive old man, a holocaust victim, with thick glasses, notorious for his view that creating greed is the clue to a thriving economy, told us he intended to show how the craving endemic to human nature was not its sin, but its salvation. With a wry smile, he said he knew very well why the students had brought him here. "To fill the villain role. Right? While you, Reverend, you'll inspire us to a vision of nonattachment. Consider the lilies of the field and all that. Given your spiritual aura, you'll have them hating me before the first night's over. Goodman, you'll be the second night's hero with that seductive posture of moral indignation you've made your trademark. But by the third day, you two are going to leave this campus despised. That's because you don't know human nature. You wouldn't want to admit it, even if you did." Sure enough, I got the students to booing Dichter that first night. The second night Goodman jumped in when Dichter took to ridiculing my beatnik friends and clinched his victory with the story of how he'd met Dichter's own beatnik son in a bar in the Village scribbling suicidal poems. The next morning, before we were interviewed on TV, Goodman said he wouldn't appear gratis for just any sponsor. When told the program was paid for by an electrical cooperative, however, he said, "Fine." That night, Dichter made his final appeal: believing us meant poverty, believing him, prosperity. He shook his head sadly: "Goodman deplores the commercial mentality, but just this morning he made a scene because he wasn't being paid for a TV interview. And then backstage this evening he said he would never have come to the conference if he'd known how small the honorarium was." Goodman leaped up. "You lying bastard! I never said that. Tell him, Delattre." I was so enraged, I could hardly speak. "Paul never—" I heard myself squeak. Dichter chuckled. "See how hard it is for a minister to lie? But true believers must hang together, right? Goodman with money on his mind? Heaven forbid. It seems my two colleagues can't admit to the truth of human nature. Least of all their own." The more Goodman and I tried to protest, the worse we looked. Students started jumping to their feet, demanding that we stop acting so righteous, admit we were just as greedy as anybody else, apologize to Dichter. After the program, Goodman cornered Dichter backstage, raging at him. Dichter shrugged: "Come on, Paul. How else would I get them to doubt that nasty stuff you said about my son? Besides, you should be grateful. I gave you both a deeper understanding of human nature. Students always start by believing the idealist. But, in the end, they put their trust in the one who justifies their greed. Remember this."

I Become a Saint

I wasn't interested in converting anybody to Christianity, but simply in providing a compassionate presence, and a place for the North Beach "beatnik" community to gather in search of the moral and spiritual dimension of their art. Lois and I served bread and wine along with coffee and spaghetti dinners to some three hundred people who trudged nightly up Telegraph Hill to come sit on our floor, listen to music and poetry, drum, but mostly just to talk. My beatnik friends jokingly (and I think lovingly) called our place "The Bread and Wine Mission." I became known as "the beatnik priest." After *Time* magazine, *Newsweek,* and the *New York Times* did feature articles on me, and cover artist Howard Brodie did a syndicated piece with me appearing in newspapers nationwide like a saint with my sweatshirt, pectoral cross, and heavenward gaze, gawkers from all over the world – not saints, but saintly people – Catholic workers from the slums of New York, underground worker priests from Eastern Europe, ministers on the experimental fringe, Hasidic rabbis, lay people from the worldwide religious community started arriving to watch the beatnik priest in action. Some of them spread the word that I just might possibly be a saint. Strangers would approach me wide-eyed, anticipating the miraculous touch of my hand. They went away sometimes "miraculously" healed. Ears were unstopped so that ordinary religious truths from my mouth were heard as astonishing revelations. The sacred energy believers invested me with was starting to make me glow—in public. As soon as I was behind closed doors with my family, I became miserable. I could feel darkness and violence growing inside of me. I knew I was a fraud. My God-given personality detested sainthood. The old Pierre Delattre with all his flaws started putting up a desperate struggle for survival against the beatnik priest. With the rebel and the saint fighting it out, my family life was bound to disintegrate. I would learn too late that whether someone is called saint, reverend mother or father, swami, babba, master, or guru, when he or she is placed above others on the pedestal where only God and the avatars belong, things will fall apart. Was it Camus who said that if God didn't exist we would have to invent a divinity to save ourselves from turning human beings into idols? Yearning for an ordinary life, my personality began to topple the idol, in a cowardly way at first, perversely doing everything in secret or in private that would destroy the image of the saint in public, but contriving, if only unconsciously, to get caught. What a relief it would be when I would finally achieve public disgrace. I kept thinking of Lao-tsu's words, "Welcome disgrace as a pleasant surprise." The surprise was due, I told myself, praying that my wife and children would not suffer too much on account of it.

The Debbie Reynolds Salad

Arthur Freed, Hollywood producer, while I'm seated across from his desk, MGM studios, Culver City, 1960: "Kerouac won't cooperate, won't even talk to us. So what Robert here has done at my suggestion is to add a swinging though entirely smoore beatnik preacher to the script of "The Subterraneans." That's why we flew you out. Surprised, huh? Of course, you wouldn't want to play yourself, nobody does that very well. We've decided to make you a kind of Protestant Bing Crosby. People flock to your religious coffeehouse to hear you grooving. You're hip. You're cool. They can talk to you. George, Leslie, Roddy, all of them dig breaking bread with you, drinking wine, telling you their problems. Mardou comes to you. That's Leslie Caron. She couldn't be here right now, but she and Roddy McDowell, they'll be out to visit you in a week or so. They want to disguise themselves as beatniks, hang around, observe. Unfortunately, George can't come. He's finishing up a New York engagement. George Peppard. Wonderful new actor. We're going to make him a star. It's George's first role. He saves Leslie. She can't be a Negro, that's too risky. We've made her French. Well, she *is* French, so that's easy. Leslie can't have a sexual what-you-call-it anymore. That's where you come in. Gerry Mulligan here, he plays you. He, that is you, you teach her love, then Leslie falls in love with George. But there's this episode with Roddy. And then, her being French now, I think it will go this way: She remembers her mother having her head shaved as a collaborator. Flashback. Terrible trauma. She comes to the Reverend Pierre Delattre, who, by the way, we've given a different name, more American, you see, his being a jazz musician. Yes, of course you're a real person, but we've thought it more authentic to call you what, Robert? This is Robert Thom. He's doing the script. And this is André Previn, he's doing the music. Terry Saunders here, the director, his brother Dennis, coproducer. We're calling Gerry . . . which is to say, we're calling you the Reverend Joshua Jones. Okay, calm down. We should go have lunch. You can think this over. Wait until you see the set. We took the liberty of photographing your place while you were on vacation. Just like home. Right. Let's all go to the cafeteria, you can think about it." We walk down a corridor past photos of stars, each of whom Freed speaks of in hushed, reverent tones. At the cafeteria, there's Frank Sinatra pasta, Gene Kelly soup on the menu. I'm about to order the Debbie Reynolds Salad when who should breeze over to our table but Debbie herself? Freed stands. "Miss Reynolds, I'd like you to meet the Reverend." She extends her hand. I, too nervous to think what I'm saying, rise, sing out, "Pleased to meet you, Miss Reynolds. I'd love to eat your salad." Her hand withdraws, she marches off. Mulligan, Thom, and the others muffle their laughter. Freed sputters: "Reverend! She's sacred in these parts!"

Making the Scene

In the office of the censor whom Robert Thom, scriptwriter, calls The Obscenity Man, a person they forgot to introduce me to sits me down. "Glad you're on board. We've been having real trouble with that boy Thom. We've come a long way to accommodate ourselves to his point of view because, believe it or not, we really do know the value of this film as a document on the early life of the beatniks. We've even gone so far as to say that George and Leslie can have sex out of marriage. But we insist that they absolutely cannot enjoy it. That's the code. To have them enjoy intercourse when they're not even married is at this point in time unthinkable here in Hollywood. Nor can they be seen riding the cable car afterward, laughing, waving balloons. What would people conclude? I said to Robert, listen, Robert, that's a horse of another feather which we simply cannot absorb. And then he goes right back and writes an even more vulgar version. Plus frankly, Reverend, we have another problem we were hoping you could help us with: Leslie comes to you because she's been traumatized. Her problem is that she can no longer have . . . I'm going to use the word bluntly and hope you won't feel offended . . . an orgasm, if I may be so blunt, forgive me if you will, I'm sorry. She can no longer have an orgasm. Now that's fine. And it's fine that she wants to have an orgasm. We don't mind. Our stand for some time is that we have absolutely nothing against the orgasm per se. But do they have to call it that? Isn't there any other way Mardou can state her problem. Isn't there some other term you beatniks use? Wait, let me write that down. Make the scene? She can't make the scene? Wonderful. That would be more than acceptable. In that context, the meaning of the word 'make' would certainly pass over the heads of children. I'm glad we brought you down. It's so good to get some authenticity straight from the horse's mouth."

Knowing Somebody

A woman phoned saying she was in town for a professional convention. She wondered if I was related to a man with the same name as mine whom she had known thirty years ago when she was sixteen. I said he was my father. She said she had met him in 1938 while working as a chambermaid in a little resort hotel on Cape Cod. She'd always wondered what happened to him. I said I didn't know he'd ever been to Cape Cod. "Oh, yes," she said. She remembered so vividly how all the guests had sat at the piano listening to him play those melancholy pieces by Schubert. "He seemed so lonely." "I didn't know my father played Schubert. All I ever heard him play was Bach and Mozart." "Oh yes. Schubert was his great love. Schubert and poetry. I remember going out and finding him seated on a rock with the surf swirling all around. He was writing those heartrending poems." I said, "I didn't think my father had any interest in poetry. He never paid attention to the poems *I* wrote. Or to my drawings." "Yes, his drawings," she said, "on little scraps of paper. I remember when I invited him to our house. My mother made us lemonade, and I lay in the hammock looking at his renderings of dunes and seabirds. He sat in the grass in his white shorts. Your father had such handsome legs." "He never told me he drew," I said. "He said nothing about the drawings I did for my book." She said, "When he took that little room next to the Y in Detroit, I went up to see him. He had his easel set up, but he was too miserable to paint. The separation, you know. Missing not being with his boys." I said, "I never knew my parents separated. I remember Dad wasn't home much that year before we moved. So you knew him in Detroit too?" "Yes, I became a student of his." I said I'd never been sure why Dad got fired from the university, though my mother had hinted at some kind of scandal involving a young girl. "Yes, after he got fired he divorced your mother, but then he landed that job in Oklahoma. On the application he'd said he was married, so he married her again for appearance' sake, don't you know." "He remarried my mother for appearance' sake?" "And I suppose he's still with her? Your mother?" "No, they're divorced." "Really. Where's he living these days?" "Down the coast." "*Is* he? I would so love to visit him, just to say hello. To be frank about it, I didn't come to San Francisco for the convention. I came to get away from my husband for a while. So, you see, I have a little time. Did you know that my husband and I taught Sunday School together for thirty years and just last week he told me he had never believed in God? Isn't that incredible? You think you know somebody." We both thought about this. Then she said, "I don't suppose your father remarried. He's not the sort." I said, "I guess I wouldn't know what sort he is. But, yes, he remarried." A pause, then, "That's all I needed to know." She slammed the phone down in my ear.

I and Thou

The so-called beats would soon be driven out of North Beach by merchants and beatniks trying to exploit them commercially. Overwhelmed by all the attention, they would mostly burn themselves out. Those who survived would either join the Vietnam War protestors and the civil-rights demonstrators in the south, go underground with the Weatherpeople or Black Panthers, or would end up as hippie flower children taking huge doses of psychedelics in the Haight. Meanwhile, my phone was ringing off the hook day and night with people in jail, in mental hospitals, calling because a friend was about to jump off a ledge or OD on something. I couldn't find enough psychiatric help. The police and newspapers became more and more hostile, though the chamber of commerce must have delighted in crowds of tourists and weekend beatniks so thick up and down Grant Avenue that you couldn't get a car through. Except during the weekend poetry reading and jam sessions at my place, I never had time to fully enjoy the tremendous melding of folk music, jazz, poetry, Zen, and life-style experimentation that was going on. From the time Bill Margolis threw himself out a window (he's in a wheelchair today, but doing well, I understand), I was rushing about from mental hospital to jail to street corner trying to deal with one casualty after another. I got so frazzled that one day I stopped hearing what people were saying; I flew into a rage and tore the telephone out of the wall. I shut our coffeehouse doors, quit the ministry, ran away, hid out in the mountains for a month, and was restored to sanity only by an insane old victim of the 1930's waterfront strike – one they called the Sandman, who had been mute since he'd been hit over the head with an iron bar. With this nearly naked red-skinned man (my *saddhu*), I too stripped down to my shorts and daily kept a fire going at Aquatic Park. I swam every day, regained my mental health. From the Sandman, I learned the healing power of water, fire, earth, and air. I started taking pleasure in being a minister again, listening to confession, but this time in the anonymous guise of a cabdriver. One day three ministers in our church, who had spent a week of intimate discussion and prayer with me up at a retreat center on Mount Tamalpais two months earlier, got into my cab, two in back, one in front. We carried on a theological discussion all the way to the airport about Martin Buber's *I and Thou* (if you see people only as tools, as objects playing roles, they will see you only that way, but if you see through their roles to the subject, and can see them as "thou," then you also become the sacred "thou" in their eyes). When the ministers got out, they tipped me well, told me condescendingly that it was amazing a cabdriver could be so articulate about Buber. After they had hurried to catch their plane, I stood there amazed to realize they hadn't recognized me.

A Strange Malady

My marriage fell apart. I lost another job, lost custody of the kids. Most of my friends had stopped speaking to me. I was down to my last hundred bucks. I left San Francisco and drove south with Carol, the woman I had disgraced myself with. We ended up in a crummy apartment in Long Beach. I got a job clerking on the docks. I was working down in the hold of a ship one morning when I began to feel strange. I couldn't figure out what was wrong. It seemed that I was getting sicker and sicker, but I couldn't locate what part of my body the disease was in. All I knew was that this bizarre uneasiness was creeping through my body – my blood or my nerves or some organ or other . . . I just couldn't locate it. Finally it got so bad I started to shake. I was getting scared. What was coming over me? I could hardly climb the ladder, my hands were so sweaty. I staggered down the gangplank, told the walking boss I was feeling really sick; he said to take a break, go sit on the end of the pier for a while, maybe I just needed some fresh air.

So I went out there and sat with my feet dangling over that oily, stinking water, wondering what was going on inside of me that was so weird . . . when it finally dawned on me. I hadn't felt this way for so long, I'd forgotten what it was like. I was happy. I scrambled to my feet and spread out my arms to the sun while the gulls flocked above me. Happiness! That's what I had! I was happy! Happy again!

The Truth in Boxing

I'm clerking for a gang of white longshoremen loading pallet boards on the waterfront, Pier 9. A little old guy with tattooed muscles is showing off, doing pushups on the handles of a dolly while another guy tells him what a great boxer he was back in the old days. "There'll never be another fighter like you," he's saying. "Yeah," says another, "the fights just ain't what they used to be when you was in the ring, kid. I remember that fight in South San Francisco when you beat Kid Sullivan. That's when a fight was a fight." "Them was the days, all right," says another. "Once they let them niggers into the ring it was all over. Jab and run, dance like a sissy, clown around. You couldn't take the fights serious no more. It was downhill all the way once they let the niggers in." While this is being said, our boxer-hero has stopped doing pushups. He's shadow boxing, bobbing and weaving, sticking a thumb to his nostril, snorting out snot. Now he's got his hands up over his face, crouched down. He starts talking in that sweet, high pitched voice all the punch-drunk fighters seem to have: "Wait a minute you guys. Hey, hey, listen, wait now, just wait a minute here. There's somethin' wrong, somethin' wrong with what you're sayin', see? Hold it. Hold it. Give me a sec, I can figure this out. Gotta think." We see him go jogging off, punching the air, shaking the cobwebs. He jogs all the way to the far end of the shed. We keep on stacking boxes onto the boards. After five minutes or so, we hear him shout, "Hey fellas, I got it! I got it!" He comes running back toward us. His hands are upraised. He's wearing a victory grin. "I know what's wrong! What's wrong with what you're saying, see? The thing is . . ." He stands in front of us panting, absolutely delighted with himself, his eyes wide with the comprehension of it: "They win! They win!"

You Write
with a Facility

When I lived in North Beach, I fantacized having my friend's job as bartender at the Coffee Gallery. The best scat and blues singers performed there; some great jazz bands playcd there. I had a lousy job working on the San Francisco docks while I tried to make it as a writer. Of course my goal was to be published, as so many of my literary heroes had been, in the *Atlantic Monthly*. My first few stories were rejected with a little slip that said something like, "Sorry, due to the many manuscripts we receive, etc. The Editors." No encouragement at all. But then I got one that said, "You write with a facility that has held our attention." For the next eight stories sent, I continued to write with this same attention-holding facility; then a better rejection slip arrived saying merely, "Thanks, please try us again," but initialed by an editor. The *Atlantic* must have had some kind of system where you never dropped back but stayed at a certain level until you were passed on to the editor of a higher category, and then you stayed there unless, after many more tries, they decided to let you rise higher. I collected ten different stages of rejection slips from the *Atlantic,* each on better paper, more finely printed, eventually signed with the full name of an editor, and then actually commented on. At last I sold an *Atlantic* First. I had been sending the magazine stories for ten years. Okay, so one day I'm walking along Fisherman's Wharf when I see my bartender friend running toward me: "Pierre, Pierre, have you heard! I've quit my job. I'm going into writing full time." I said, "Are you kidding? Quit the best job in town? What for?" "I've had some tremendous encouragement from the *Atlantic Monthly.* They love me. They wrote me this wonderful letter. I'm practically in. It means I'm off at last on a really serious literary career." "Jesus Christ, what did they say?" "Pierre, oh shit, you won't believe this. They say I write with a *facility* that has held their *attention!*"

Courage

During the three years I worked on the San Francisco waterfront, I observed that you weren't really accepted as part of the in-group of clerks and longshoremen until the walking boss addressed you in a thoroughly insulting way. The International Longshoremen's and Warehousemen's Union had grown so powerful that much of what we did was look-busy fake labor: moving pallet boards from one end of the warehouse to the other and back again; sending twelve men into the hold to do the work of three while the other nine got out their knives and practiced the art of pilfering. The result is that we took little pride in our work. As we observed the efficiency of the Japanese when they came into port, we could imagine how they loaded their ships back home, and we began to feel, in fact, ashamed. This was reflected in the contemptuous way we addressed one another. But there was a hierarchy to insult. The first time the walking boss called me a no good, fucking, cocksucking son of a bitch, I was thrilled. It meant I belonged. But

I never would have spoken such words to him, only to another ordinary laborer like myself. I especially would not have cursed Donovan, who was the meanest walking boss on the docks. That is why I and all the guys within hearing distance dropped what we were doing and listened amazed to the voice of a guy we called Mighty Mouse as he finally lost it with Donovan, a man whose abuse he had sworn he would not put up with anymore. "Listen, Donovan," we heard him scream, "you goddam, fucking son of a bitch. You give me any more trouble, I'm going to stick this hook right through your neck. You cocksucking, motherfucking no-good excuse for a walking boss, you think you're shit on a stick, you're nothing but a big fat fart on a log. You hear me? I want to see you treat the guys who actually work around here with more respect from now on, or we're going to pick your ass up and throw you into the fucking drink." We listened amazed. This was wonderful! What guts! All of us dropped what we were doing and ran down the dock to where our hero's voice was coming from. There behind a stack of bales we found him with his face right up to that of his best buddy. "That's what I'm going to tell him!" he was screaming. "That's what I'm going to tell him!"

An Acting Lesson

I was stage-managing *Escuriel,* a play by Michel de Ghelderode about a king who asks the jester to amuse him by donning his king's garments and sitting on the throne while he, the king, takes on the role and garments of the fool. Playing king, the fool gets carried away and accuses his supposed fool of having an affair with the queen, offering enough evidence so that the fool who is really the king breaks down and confesses. The real king then sheds his fool's garments, reclaims the throne and, reminding the real fool that, after all, he (the king — are you following?) does possess the power, calls for the executioner, who strolls in wearing a black hood and strangles the true fool on the spot. Curtain. One sold-out night, the guy who played the executioner called in sick only an hour before curtain time. I said I could play the executioner, no problem. Bob Elross, the director, said I hadn't been in his acting classes long enough to know how to carry off such a difficult role. "Hell," I said, "all I have to do is go out and strangle the guy." "That's all?" Bob laughed. "You're talking about Bruce Maki, the best actor we've ever had in this theater. You think you can play against a guy of his caliber?" "Why not?" I said, "All he has to do is get strangled by me, fall down and die. How can I miss? I don't speak any lines." "Uh-huh," said Bob. "So, go put on your robe and mask, schmuck." I stood backstage through this long one-acter, eager to go out and do my bit of histrionics. When Bob (playing the king) finally summoned me, I stepped out of the wings. Bob pointed to Bruce. "Kill him!" he shouted. I strode toward Bruce, reaching for his neck. Though I was taller than he was, he had only to catch me by the thumb and wrist to flip me head over heels and bring me crashing down on stage. The audience roared with laughter. "Idiot! Kill him!" Bob screamed. Humiliated, I struggled to my feet, rushed at Bruce. This time I got my hands around his throat, but he got his around mine as well. He was surprisingly strong. I gagged, broke away, charged at him again. We wrestled. The audience cheered the fool. The king went into a rage. The boos and hisses grew louder and louder. I felt horribly embarrassed. I glanced past the footlights. Some people in the audience were on their feet, egging Bruce on. I knew I had to kill him at any cost or be the disgrace of the whole troupe, the spoiler before our largest audience ever. Shrieking with genuine anguish, I sprang at him. Ignoring a blow to my guts, tears wetting my mask, I finally got both my hands solidly around his neck and brought him crashing down. His head snapped back. He fell dead. I staggered off stage as the curtain dropped to wild and sustained applause. It had taken me fifteen minutes to kill Bruce. He shook my hand between curtain calls. "Not bad," he said. "You might turn out to be a real actor some day."

Refusal of the Gift
Is the Beginning of Evil

In the biblical story, Abel's gift was accepted and, presumably, Abel would have gone on to become a good man. But Cain's gift was rejected, so he slew his brother. Working with young people, I could see that rejection of their gifts was indeed a major cause of unhappiness and rage. Yet in our families, our school systems, our churches, in fact in all our social gatherings, the people who can come to us with a problem will almost always be able to claim precedence over those who merely come offering a gift. We can deal with the problematical. It makes us feel superior and in control to listen to the miseries of others. We can condescend to them by worrying about them and feeling blessed by our relative good fortune. We can also make good money off of them; and by picking at the dis-ease, we can keep it lucratively festering. When they bring us their creative vision, we have a much harder time. Receiving a gift humbles us, since all creative work shakes the foundations of our confidence, reminds us of our dependency, and forces us to open ourselves once more to the mystery of grace. In our schools, programs for the gifted are always the first to be cut so as to accommodate the children with "problems." Pretty soon, the wise creative child learns how to stop being ignored by becoming problematical. When I opened up my storefront coffeehouse, I was resolved to encourage the artistic and spiritual gifts of a community moving against the mainstream of American culture. But soon I had no time for the gifted. Despite my best intentions, I simply could not turn away from the endless up-front, hand-waving, weeping-on-the-phone, "I-must-interrupt you-right-now!" immodesty and outright bullying of people who had come to expect that attention belonged, by the right of supreme misery, to them. After I left North Beach, the Presbyterian church let me set up an arts center in an abandoned church in the Mission district. But when the ministers working with addicts and the mentally ill saw all the happiness in our theaters and galleries, they demanded that most of our funding be cut and turned over to them. They suddenly discovered that our building was crucial to their social work; they took over the downstairs, demanded that we approach our art in terms of discussion groups after every show about "the problem of modern man." Again the problematical approach swarmed over and drowned out any devotion to the gifted. My friends in the liberal clergy always seemed to feel ill at ease with creative people until their troubles were uncovered; then they felt comfortable again, at home in the familiar territory of that creed that said there is no health in us and we are all miserable offenders. Much as I appreciated and had participated in the efforts at improving civil rights and the social good, the artist in me felt a need to escape from the Church in order to follow a more spiritually creative path. And so I did.

The Golden Gate Swim

Forty men were jumping up and down in the fog at dawn on Baker's Beach, ready to make the swim from the San Francisco to the Marin County side. Once we were out there in the choppy waters of the "potato patch," just outside the Golden Gate Bridge, we knew we would be quickly scattered; a few guys on paddleboards would be skimming about, but essentially we would be on our own. We were trying not to think about the girl who had been bitten in half by a shark just off that beach the year before. John, our swim captain, explained that we were entering at ebb tide. If we swam straight forward, the tide would start moving in soon, and we would be carried under the bridge at an angle to Lime Point off the Sausalito coast where a ferryboat awaited us. We charged into the waves. Within minutes I found myself swimming in rough water with not another orange Day-Glo cap in sight. I had learned my lesson from an excruciating cramp just before I'd reached shore during the Alcatraz swim. You can't tense up or it's over.

The challenge is to the mind and spirit. If I stayed relaxed my un-greased body would endure the estimated hour and ten minutes. Indeed the first half hour felt terrific. After having kept my composure during a scrape with driftwood that I'd thought was a shark, I already felt victorious. The only thing that troubled me was that the tide hadn't turned yet. In fact, even when I swam more at an angle inward toward the bridge, it seemed I was being carried out to sea. Then I saw man on a paddleboard gliding toward me. He said John had done this incredibly stupid thing. He had called the tide wrong. It was going out, not in. "Grab the board and I'll tow you to a boat." I heard myself say, "No, I can make it." I refused to take hold. With no more time to argue, he skimmed away in search of others. What had I done? I could already visualize the sharks and little fish nibbling at my drowned flesh. I remembered saying to my wife, Lois, that arguing about custody of the kids was too painful; it would be better if one of us was dead. Apparently I had just decided it should be me. I yielded briefly to terror, shivering violently, but got the hypothermia under control, told God I'd changed my mind, begged to be saved, despaired, then accepted my death, and glided into a serene calm. I breaststroked onward, seeing myself getting closer to the lighthouse and the open sea. I was swimming on what I now blissfully knew was the belly of the great mother when I heard the roaring of a riptide, which, I hadn't been aware, flows up the shore as the tide moves out. I entered this countercurrent and was swept at amazing speed under the shadow of the bridge all the way to Lime Point. Cheered by the rescued men on the ferryboat, I climbed the ladder and stood on deck in the exhilarating wind, knowing that I had given death his chance. He had rejected me. I could start a new life. Two years later, it was Lois who tempted death, and was taken.

I Am Given Directions
to the Virgin of Guadalupe

The guy behind the desk had asked why I'd left my job. I said I'd stopped believing in God. It wasn't true, but how else could I explain leaving the ministry. He said, "I can't give you unemployment benefits for that." I'd tried the employment agencies. Nobody wanted to spoil the fun by hiring an ex-clergyman. Back in San Francisco, desperate for money, I'd agreed to play a cameo role in a movie Fred Hobbs was making. Fred had thought it fun to cast me as a lascivious priest, a caricature of my former self who opens his fly and lets his penis flower into a rose as his chair rises on a pole until he's looking way down on the girl confessing her sins. I'd gone along with this, wondering how I could mock a profession I had sincerely given my life to for so long. Years later, I knocked on the door of Fred's studio in the Mission district, again desperate for a quick-money role. It was raining; I was cold. Down the street, I saw the marquee at the burlesque theater: "Final Night at the Follies." I decided I'd go take refuge there, then try Fred again. The theater was packed, but I got a seat up front by making a guy remove his coat from a chair. The star stripper strutted out onto the ramp and said how sorry she was to be ending her career on the burlesque stage. She wanted to give us something special tonight. She had understood long ago that we didn't come to see her so much out of lust as out of religious longing. She asked where else you could go to worship the feminine? She said she'd remained a virgin all these years so that all of us could love and worship her equally. She showed us a feather duster, said she wanted each of us to brush her pussy with it. Quickly, men began to line up down the central aisle. She lay back, spread her legs, raised her head and watched as each man revently took the duster from the man in front of him and had his turn at brushing it against her beautiful pink labia while she gave a little shriek. I watched this ceremony with awe, though I was too shy to take my place in line. When all were back in their seats, she told us to unzip. She wanted to make us come in unison. Men all around me took their penises in hand. She stood up; she peered down at us. "That's the way, that's it." When her eyes fell on me she said, "What about you?" I shrugged. "Oh dear," she said. "If you can't join the others, there's something really wrong. You better leave. Go search elsewhere for the goddess." I got up to jeers and catcalls. As I was edging my way past the penises, she shushed the men: "That's all right. He'll find her in his own way, won't he? I have it!" She lowered her voice to a whisper. "Let him go find her in Mexico. There's another virgin there, more pure than I am. She's the one for him." I did leave for Mexico. And I did find the Virgin of Guadalupe, a goddess I could worship.

Bargaining with Lola

I was told that Doña Lola didn't want to rent the crumbling colonial house I lusted after in San Miguel – with its pink arches, fruit trees in the patio, high-ceilinged rooms, magnificent fireplaces – because she was in her eighties now and wanted to feel free to return to the place of her birth when it was her time to die. Nevertheless, I took the long bus trip to Mexico City, was ushered by a maid into Lola's apartment. This enormous bullfrog of a woman was wedged into the window seat, watching the mariachis in a park below. She asked me to state my business, said the house was absolutely not for rent. "Hear me out," I said, and made my proposal: If she would rent me the house I would keep in reserve the bedroom in which she had been born so that she could come there any time she felt in danger of dying. Intrigued, she bade me come sit across from her in the window seat. We faced off knee to knee. "You would let me go there to die any time I pleased?" "Any time, Doña Lola. We could put it in the contract." "Even if it turned out I didn't die, in which case I would come back here to Mexico City? Because when my death is certain I would not want you in my house anymore? Just when my death is in question—as a possibility. Understand?" "Yes, I understand perfectly. And since there is no certainty of your dying for . . . at least ten years, I propose a lease of no longer than that." She tugged her dress up over her blue-black swollen knees. "Are these the knees of a woman who's going to live another ten years? I give myself a year at the most." "Your cheeks are as rosy as a young girl's, Doña Lola. I give you eight years without question." "That's because you don't know rouge when you see it, *cabrón*. Two maybe." I said, "I give you seven for sure." She scoffed. "Three at the most." I rolled my eyes. "I would bet my last peso that you will be alive three and a half years from now *à lo menos*." She kicked my shin. "Don't flatter me, gringo. Three is final. And you pay for repairs." I agreed. She seized my hands, brought them warmly to her breast, shook them. We were brought coffee and *pan dulce*. I wrote up the contract; we signed it. Every eight or nine months, Lola and her maid would arrive from Mexico City in a cab, stay a few weeks while her local friends brought food, drink, and flowers, and waited for her to die. Once past the death mood, Lola would apologize for the false alarm and return to the city. Lola taught us the secrets of her house: about how the Spanish gentleman, for example, who used to serenade her at the window, was shot after the revolution, and became the same ghost my partner Carol and I had seen walk past our bed, stop startled when he saw us, and return in confusion to the *sala;* about *la Llorona* wailing in the park up the street. After our second lease ended, Lola moved in permanently, and lasted another four years.

Nagged to Life

In San Miguel the police would put strychnine out on the streets about once a year to kill the stray dogs. The next morning the curs could be seen everywhere dead or staggering about in convulsions. Dog owners were warned to keep their pets at home on those days. My dog Lolla got out somehow. I ran about searching for her, but didn't find her until the next morning. She was lying against the wall of the post office, shuddering, her eyes glazed. Her fur was wet and cold. I carried her to the vet. We poured something down her throat that made her vomit a few blades of the strychnine, but she didn't improve. We could barely feel a pulse. And then the vet said he was sorry, her heart had stopped. I had read a story in a women's magazine the day before entitled "I Scolded My Husband Back from the Dead." It was written by a woman who got her husband's heart to restart by shouting into his ear that he had no right to die; he better come back this minute if he knew what was good for him. The husband later testified that he'd already left his body and was on his way to a happier place, but his wife's voice so terrified him that he returned to life just to appease her. I shouted into Lolla's ear, "Lolla! Come here! Come back here this minute!" Her body gave a jolt. Her tail twitched. A paw wiggled. I carried her home. She was blind for six months, had a stillborn pup, but eventually returned to full health. From that experience, I've learned that you can just as easily be nagged to life as nagged to death.

Cuauhtémoc
the Francophile

I had never seen anyone who looked so purely Aztec as the kid shining my shoes in the Toluca plaza. I asked if he knew where we could find a blind man with features like his, explaining that my Belgian partner and I were shooting a film about a man who, having failed to have his blindness healed at the shrine of Guadalupe, decides to return to the old gods, to make an offering at the sacred lake of the sun fifteen thousand feet high, inside the volcanic crater of the Toluca mountain. The boy said his name was Cuauhtémoc; he was a direct ancestor of the great prince; he would find us such a man if we'd hire him to assist. He said his French was as good as ours. We pretended to believe him and took him on. Cuauhtéhmoc found us a blind accordionist playing outside the bus station. We filmed him first buying mangos at the market, which almost got us killed by a mob of angry Indians who saw the camera as an assault weapon on their souls. Having saved our lives with a speech in the Indian tongue, the kid got us into the van and asked if we could stop by his house to pick up some blankets. All this time we were speaking only Spanish with him. But when we got to his house, his father, an equally Aztecan little man, came out to greet us speaking French, not at first to us, but to his son. He took us into the bedroom where he said he and Cuauhtéhmoc lay every night side by side reading French novels in the comfy four-poster bed. The father, once a sailor, had spent much time in French ports, becoming a Francophile. He'd taught his son French. The two of them had read all of Balzac, Proust, Flaubert, Stendhal. Their insights into these novels astonished us. After the father kissed us on both cheeks, then got to work on copies of French paintings he sold for a living, we drove to the top of the Toluca volcano, staying in the guard post. At that height it took only a little brandy to get us all drunk. Cuauhtémoc expounded brilliantly his notion that Stendhal's hero Julien Sorel was the opposite of what he thought a hero should be. This twelve-year-old boy said that his great aim was not to acquire fame and fortune but, like his father, to divest himself of anything that complicated his life or kept him from enjoying art and literature for its own sweet sake. The blind man got so drunk that he didn't walk down into the volcano. Grabbing fistfuls of the wonderfully unfamiliar snow, he pressed it to his face, ate it, finally rolled giggling all the way down, head over heels, almost to the lake. Holding mangos uplifted in each hand, face upraised, he cried out to the sun for sight. When he wasn't healed, nothing would persuade him to act as if he were unless we paid him twice as much money. So we did, and drove back down the mountain, the blind man angry to have made a movie that was untrue, Cuauhtémoc eager to return to the bed of his father inside that little cave of French fiction.

Death Uninterrupted

After my dog Lolla was poisoned by strychnine a second time, she didn't seem to want to go through the agony of the long recovery again. I was keeping her bedded down near the fireplace. But every time I went into another room she would get up and drag her body into the backyard, lying down under the peach tree and somehow covering herself with dead leaves. I'd go out, brush her off, pick her up, and carry her back to where it was warm. One time I returned from talking on the phone to find that she had made it only as far as the steps into the garden, where she'd collapsed. I decided not to try to save her anymore. I carried her out to the peach tree and lay her down. She let me know that she didn't want me to stay too close to her. She didn't want to be touched or talked to. She just wanted me nearby. So I sat on the steps and watched while she wiggled into the leaves, a maneuver she seemed to know by instinct. When her body was entirely covered, except for her snout — which was pointing directly at the late afternoon sun shining there on her from over the fence – she lay quietly alert. Just as the sun set, she gave off a shudder that shook away the leaves. I saw a pale silver glow surround her. The glow lasted for about fifteen minutes, faded away, and left her body quite dead. I dug the grave there under the tree. From Lolla I learned once again that dying is a solitary act of enormous spiritual concentration that should not be disturbed by our tears and words of grief or consolation. The best we can do for dying creatures, human or animal, is to let them connect somehow with the earth and then to guard them so that they can die uninterrupted.

A Field of
Sombreros Popping

When we arrived, a small band was playing under a tree in a dirt corral about the size of a football field. The corral was surrounded by a stone fence upon which hundreds of young buck rancheros dressed in shiny pastel shirts and yellow plastic sombreros sat shoulder to shoulder. Two tin chairs had been placed at the center of the corral. Several of the girls, who had gathered around the bride near a long adobe building, escorted us to the chairs then returned to their group. We sat stiffly. A murmur arose from the bucks. Carol kept saying no, she wasn't going to get up and dance in front of all these people. "We have to," I said. I dragged her to a standing position. The bucks whistled approval. Carol smiled politely, said, "I'm not dancing, asshole." I said, "We have to dance, goddamit." "Not until somebody else does," she whispered. I said with a smile, "If we don't, they don't. So you better dance, bitch." She looked up me lovingly and said, "Fuck you. You never could lead me in a two-step. And don't you go showing off any of that improvised stuff either." I let go of her, made a few fancy moves. The girls shrieked. Carol said to hell with it, and started to boogie. The young bucks aye-aye-ayed. They began crossing the field to go find a partner. All the couples tried to outclass us. Pretty soon the dance was going great guns. It was time to go thank our maid, Lola, for inviting us. We found her in a blackened room pungent of chocolate and chile. She was stirring chicken mole in a gigantic pot. She sent us to sit with other guests at a long table. They drank Pepsi; we were served beer. Others had small portions; ours were huge. When we staggered from the table, others would enter until all were fed. In a dark bed-room, the bride was waiting with her girlfriends to learn all she could from the gringa about sex. The men called me to their corner, opened beers. The groom pulled a basket from under the bed, unwrapped a bottle of clear liquid from a serape, poured me a tall glass right to the brim. Noblesse oblige; I chugalugged pure fire; my brain blossomed. Soon I was making jokes with the others, roaring my head off. Three leathery old men with thick white eyebrows entered wearing the crusty sombreros of authentic revolutionaries. Everyone fell silent and stood. The men and women kissed their hands. I was the only one just to shake hands in that soft, palm-to-palm, gently touching way of the cam-pesino. Another glass of the magic mescal was poured for the grand-fathers and me. Our eyes laughed, we shrugged at our foolishness, and downed it. I heard Carol on the bed resume instructions on how to in-sert a diaphragm she had smuggled to the bride. I staggered out and danced under a single electric light hanging from a tree at the edge of the corral. While I leaped and spun, I kept seeing this huge field of sombreros popping up and down: Thousands of men jumping to catch a glimpse of the crazy gringo dancing.

Calling the Cows
and Other Spirits

Sitting in meditation in a cave behind a waterfall high up a canyon outside of San Miguel above the swimming hole that I visited so often, I heard a radio playing, then saw a boy of about sixteen, a shepherd dressed more or less as I had dressed when I was a herder of cows on my grandfather's farm. I saw this barefooted young man scramble down the path, set his radio on a rock, shed his straw hat and overalls, and, before I had time to let him know that I was watching, dive into the water. I decided the best thing was not to move and hope he'd leave without seeing me; I didn't want to scare the hell out of him, seated as I was in my lotus behind the weave of water and dangling vines. He splashed about for a time, then clambered out, shook the water from his hair, turned off his radio, leaned back looking up to the tops of the cliffs, cupped his hands to his mouth, and began to scream out the names of all the girls he must have longed to make love with. In Mexico, almost all campesina girls add the name of the virgin to the front of their names: Maria Doloreees!" he screamed. "Maria Conchaaa! Maria Lourdeees!" On and on their names echoed against the canyon walls until, gathering all his forces, he cried out with delirious joy the name given to the daughter of the whore: "Hija de la chingadaaaaaaaaaaa!" Then he got dressed, picked up his radio and was gone. He reminded me of how I used to stand with my brother near the salt lick, behind the barn in Wisconsin calling out the names of the cows. If we called each one in proper order, leading off with Ollie the bell cow, we didn't have to go after them; they'd come walking in line down the hill, their bags full, ready to be milked. But if we called any cow out of turn, that one would go sulk way up in woods of the back forty. When we went up and finally found her, she would look at us with a huge, accusing eye, making us throw a stone before she'd move, and then she'd run too fast, spoiling the creamy sweetness of her milk. The Mexican shepherd boy awakened a longing to return to the farm of my deceased grandparents, so I did. It took three days and four nights on the bus. My brother, who took care of the farm, was not there. I walked from the farmhouse, past the barn and through the woods along the lake to the cottage, cleaned it up, and climbed into the attic to get rid of a squirrel. Under a floorboard, I discovered a tin box in which my grandfather had stashed away a stack of photos of women taking coquettish poses. They were farm women. In one photo, he had two of them seated on his knees as he sat on a stump. In another, he sat with three of them on the sauna steps. He had written their names on the back: Ollie, Tillie, Nellie, Gertie, Betsy, Peggy... the very names of the cows my brother and I had called forth from their grazing during the summer dawns of our youth. What a kick my grandfather must have gotten out of that.

Capturing the Image

An Indian, whom I'd photographed in a Mexican market without asking his permission, grabbed my camera and spat at me. A hostile crowd gathered. The enraged man smashed the camera underfoot. I didn't protest, but walked away feeling lucky not to have been killed. I knew I'd been foolish, since I was well acquainted with the Indians' belief that you can capture a person's soul in a photograph. Only a week later, I would learn that it was even more than that: black-and-white photographs have a way of revealing a dark side of life that direct vision refuses to see. With my lover Carol, I returned from Mexico, took a hotel room, and walked alone to my wife Lois and the children's new apartment on Christmas morning. We tried to make it like old times, opening presents under the tree, then having french pancakes and cocoa in the kitchen. Despite the pain of old memories and new regrets, the charade of still being a family was going well enough until my son's pal Chris arrived to show off his present, a Polaroid Instamatic camera. He wanted Lois and me to pose together, but we weren't a couple anymore, and neither of us could bear the pain of such pretense, so we told Chris to take separate shots of us. I asked Chris if I could hold the one he took of Lois so that I could see the magic of the image gradually emerging. The kids had run off to the other room. I was seated on a kitchen chair in the freshly painted, cheerful little kitchen. Lois at the stove was convincing me of how happy she was with her new boyfriend, and I was believing it, for she seemed to me more radiant and healthy than I'd seen her in years, her blue eyes crystal clear, her cheeks exceptionally rosy, lips especially red, those thick eyebrows blacker than ever, and her hair thicker. The photo in my lap was gradually turning from black to brown as her image congealed. When it had fully solidified, terror struck my heart, followed by an immense sorrow. Lois in the photo was mercilessly revealed in the full misery of her being, an unhappiness so extreme that I could hardly bear to look. What I saw, now that she was reduced to black and white, was her death; I saw that she was living beyond hope, on the other side of despair. Her ravaged expression said that she had given up on life; and that this cheerful act of hers – as she served me what had been traditional Sunday breakfast during our wonderful ten years of marriage preceding a breakup neither of us understood – was a final act of love or compassion put on for my sake, despite all the pain I'd caused her. I set the photo aside, quickly ate my breakfast, got up, embraced her and the children, and, saying that I had to rush to catch my bus, fled the apartment. I hastened to the room where Carol was waiting, told her we were taking the next bus back to Mexico. Nineteen days later, Lois was dead.

Suffer the Children

I found the children at Michele's best friend Cynthia's house watching television, and was amazed at how calm they seemed over their mother's death two days earlier. We took a walk down Telegraph Hill. Recently three astronauts had died on the launching pad. To counter any horror stories they might hear later about their mother dying of a drug overdose, I said she was also a pioneer, a heroine of inner space; she had died while experimenting with journeys of the mind. This seemed to comfort them. They said they knew she would have wanted her ashes scattered on Mount Tamalpais but that Grandpa had gotten hold of the body before I'd been able to return from Mexico. He'd taken it to Visalia, where Lois's mother was buried, and that was good too – good for Grandpa. But I must go to the funeral with them. Though I dreaded it, I said I would. And a few days later the three of us were entering the funeral chapel in that valley town. We found ourselves standing before corrugated doors. The mortician pressed a button. The doors whined opened with a blast of lilac scent. On the altar was a battleship-gray casket. We sat in one of the pews and stared at this casket while others arrived, scattering in groups here and there. The organist commenced one of those tear-jerking hymns. Marc began to sob, and then Michele. I grabbed them by the hand, took them outside. Standing on the corner in the sunshine, I told them their mother wasn't up there in that casket. What they were looking at was the kind of horror show Lois wouldn't even have let them watch on TV. "Death returns us to nature is what she believed," I reminded them. No sooner had I said this than a marvelous event took place. I recognized it later when reading about the Buddha's vision of nirvana, and I remembered it from a time when a dying yogi had held my hand–how the air seemed filled with song, with falling petals, with the glory of the universe glistening. It happened just like that to the three of us as we walked around the block without saying a word. We could feel Lois's presence shining around us, singing in every tree, leaf, and flower. When we were back at the chapel, Marc said, "Let's go back in for Grandpa's sake." We decided we could survive the sermon–which indeed proved morbid–if we ignored it by playing a game. We each tried to guess how many squares there were on the upholstery that covered the back of the pew in front of us. Marc came closest. He snuck me a smile of satisfaction. Driving home, I felt tremendous relief at the way the children sang songs from *The Wizard of Oz* with all the joy of the days when the four of us would travel to Visalia. Unaware of the irony (for they were knowing and celebrating their mother's presence at that moment with all their hearts) they sang loudest of all, "Hey ho, the wicked witch is dead." How wonderfully innocent children are, I thought; how wonderfully pure in the midst of tragedy.

Incarnation

I'd read a few books on yoga, so I knew there were seven *chakras* belonging to our subtle body, located up the spine, each radiating *prahnic* energy. I could not accept the *chakras* as more than symbols, however, since Western science had made only the most dubious recordings of them. But after the night I was accidentally fed poison, I would remember how the spasms that were flinging my body about on the floor occurred in regular series of six. My mind's eye could clearly see them like fireballs blasting up my spine – bang! bang! – from one electric supercharger to the next, until . . . pow! Off I sailed through the top of my head. I found myself looking down on a scene where two people with voices like dolls were having a panicked discussion about my body being ice cold, my breathing undetectable; they could find no pulse. Because my wife had died a year earlier – victim of psychedelic missionaries – I realized, with the kind of intellectual clarity the mind can enjoy only when the senses are shutting themselves down, that I must return to my body so that our children would not have to live with the anguish of having lost both parents the same way. Up ahead, the guides were calling. I can't remember who they were, but they were wonderful people come to get me, and in a hurry, urging me not to linger. I wanted to go with them, but my mind said, "Be responsible. Get back in your body." I tried to connect to the frantic voices of the people below. No luck. Then Carol began speaking to me. At that moment, I finally understood how much she loved me, and that without this love there would have been no way of getting back into my body. I got the message that love is an incarnating force that grounds us to the material plane, and that I must take hold of the love in Carol's voice as if it were a rope down which I could slide back into my body. Heeding the faint resonance of her words so musically entering my ear, vibrating the cord up and down my spine, I took hold of this cord quickened by love and descended through the top of my head until I reached my heart, which started up with a jolt. After a rest, I descended to the region of my stomach and was able to vomit the poison. A month later I joined a yoga class. The instructor said that if we didn't discover the powers of the *chakras* earlier, we would surely do so when we died, because we'd feel our life force blasting upward from one to the other, *"shushum!"*, directly up the center into the white light. Having just experienced this, I now knew that the *chakras* were more than symbolic, and that their subtle light could be grounded only by that cord ascending and descending through the center of each body, kept resonating by the voices of our lovers. Later, in New Mexico, I would learn that the ladder into the *kiva* is the *chakric* column of a tribal body that incarnates itself downward into earth-love with chant, foot, and drumbeat.

The Last Beatnik Casualty
Is Brought to My Door

I couldn't escape the casualties of the beat generation. They kept calling me back to the Bay Area, my own wife among them, and then appearing at my door in Mexico. The last of them was Neal Cassady, hero of Kerouac's *On the Road,* the book that had made a romance of it all. The police knocked at my door saying they had a corpse in their truck; my address was in his pocket. Neal's death summed up for me what had gone wrong. Speed. We had all tried to achieve enlightenment too fast, just as we were burning up fuel while driving too fast, wasting our resources too quickly, and ourselves getting wasted in hopes of coming face to face with the ultimate before the bomb ended it all for everyone. Too many zombies with an unspoken faith in the apocalypse were looking down from the cliffs at Big Sur. And here was the body of Neal who used to rap for us, making brilliant connections between every conceivable subject past, present, and to come. There was some kind of awesome connection between his brain and tongue that seemed to make it unnecessary for him to think before he spoke. Just as he drove faster than thought when we were in the car with him ripping down the mountain, so he rapped, staying well ahead of reflection so that we could only flash on it for a second, shout "far out!", and . . . zap!, as rapidly forget. One of his girlfriends told me that he fucked like a piston for hours at a time without ever coming, then he collapsed. That seemed to be Neal's and all the speedsters' problems: they were trying to reach the end as fast as they could. As I walked along the railroad track where he collapsed for the last time on a mixture of speed and tequila, I remembered his telling me that he was tired of being a cult figure; he just wanted to go back to working on the railroad like his father. I said good-bye to his blazing spirit, and to all manner of speed in my life there and then. I decided I wanted to burn a slow flame, and last a long time. Seen from the slow perspective of a saunterer, life was too beautiful to give up on so soon.

The Bright Eye

A llow me to introduce myself," said a portly gentleman at the next table. "Doctor Mario Gonzales-Ulloa. Aesthetic plastic surgeon. I like to see if I can identify people's professions by their profile. May I venture a guess?" He scrutinized my face. "You're a writer." "Ah," I said, closing the notebook I had been writing in. He studied me further. "A writer of . . . humorous, perhaps mystical tales. A bit the philosopher, but more the theologian. Am I right?" I blushed. "Well then," he said, "may I now be allowed to predict that you and I are destined to become collaborators." I gave him my address. Three days later there was a knock on my door. Beside a Rolls-Royce stood a liveried chauffeur with the classic face of a Mayan prince. I was driven to a new house Dr. Mario had just purchased to add to numerous casas large and "chica" that he owned all over Mexico, including the hacienda outside Cuernavaca built by Cortez. I spent much time at his various homes visiting with him, his brilliant Swiss wife, his enormous entourage of artists, politicians, courtesans, children, and his two Great Danes, whom he allowed, without blinking, to slurp the steaks and chops right off our dinner plates. I translated and rewrote his books on the aesthetics of plastic surgery. Dr. Mario was dedicated to the psychic recuperation of people whose repulsive appearances caused negative energy to penetrate them from the reactions of coworkers and passersby on the street. A crowd of his formerly ugly and morose adulators held a feast once a month to lavish gifts upon him and to sing his praises for making them so beautiful, so radiantly happy that they now had lovers, sycophants, even sometimes movie contracts. Dr. Mario had no interest in creating a beautiful mask, but in releasing what he called "the bright eye." He insisted that light was not released by the eye per se, but by the many little muscles around the eyes. His specialty was the repair and training of these muscles for fluid expression. His goal: to make the entire body a beautiful, expressive work of surgical art. He said that art in stone and metal was destined to be left behind by the art of flesh. At his swank clinic in the Zona Rosa, he took me to a room where a woman lay under a sheet smiling up with adoration. I recognized her face immediately from the art books. She was rapturously beautiful. He told her he was going to pull back the sheet to show his masterpiece to his colleague. She beamed as he explained how this dear lady's flesh only weeks ago had been sagging in folds all the way from forehead to pubis. He said the woman had wanted to look like Boticelli's Venus. It was uncanny how perfectly he had fulfilled her wish – the long legs, early Renaissance bottle-hips, high little breasts, straight nose, everything! "Isn't our Mario brilliant," cried Venus, springing from the table to embrace us.

Shoulder Sex

I was in the aisle seat of a bus in Mexico City, next to a dozing campesino, taking the long lurching ride down Insurgentes from the Reforma to San Angel. All the seats were full, but there was still nobody standing when a young, nice-looking couple in their early twenties – he in a shiny suit and she in a silky green dress – boarded the bus at the front, strolled halfway back to where I sat, and took their positions side by side, each holding the ceiling rail. He was standing just in front of me; she, right at my shoulder. I glanced up at them, but neither of them took notice of me; they stared straight ahead. Two or three stops later, the aisle had become crowded, but the couple had not moved back. They stayed just where they were as the press of passengers shoved through behind them. A few more stops and we were jam-packed. I felt the young woman press herself against my shoulder, pulling her buttocks in to allow a fat man to pass. Since the part of her body that was touching me was just there at the cleft of her legs, I was sure that she would quickly disengage herself. But she kept that soft mound of Venus pressed against me. I remained as I had been, the polite gringo appearing not to notice. She began to rub against my shoulder in a small, circular motion that was so subtle at first that I couldn't quite be sure whether I wasn't just imagining what was going on. But then the rubbing became more blatant. And, I must confess, more enjoyable. I opened the book I'd been holding; I made a valiant effort at pretending to read, but my eyes, ears, nose, and throat were wide open to other possibilities. The rubbing had become so urgent that it was very hard (forgive the pun) to keep my shoulder from actively participating. I glanced up at the man beside the woman and saw that he didn't know or was pretending not to know what she was doing. Nevertheless, in deference to him, I didn't allow my hot and bothered shoulder even the slightest churning. I think it must have been her heat that filled the whole bus with such a pungent fragrance as she continued to rub herself against me for perhaps fifteen minutes. All the while, my shoulder was growing hotter and hotter . . . until I felt a sudden stopping of her motion, then a tightening of her thighs around my shoulder. Her spasm sent a warm flow down from her crotch, through my heart, into the region beneath my book. She and I and the bus all shuddered at once as we pulled up at the corner and screeched to a stop. She and her companion hurried to get off. As the bus pulled away, I leaned forward past my dozing seat partner to see what they were doing. They were standing on the curb looking just as tired and bored as everyone else.

The Greater Heart
of a Dog

N anny entered our lives when she was six weeks old, nursing a hernia she'd been born with. She was a purebred Newfy of exceptional stock. I put a mat for her beside my bed. She flopped right down, looking very happy to have found a home. In the morning she was lying there, but with a dead kitten between her paws. I was horrified. Our mother cat had just given birth to a litter of kittens out there in a corner of the patio. I gave Nanny a scolding, dragged her out, showed her the kittens, and told her never to go near them. The next night, again a dead kitten lay between Nanny's paws, a big hole chewed in its neck. She was licking the corpse. I rolled up a newspaper, gave Nanny a few whacks. I screamed at her never to do that again. How did she respond? By wagging her tail. This made me furious. I kept on berating her until I finally had her cowering in a corner. The next night, I kept the living room door shut. Around three in the morning, she started whining, jumping at the door. I put her on a choke chain and took her outside. She led me to the garden in back where, by flashlight, we found our mother cat's year-old son chewing a hole in the neck of another of the kittens. I realized that Nanny had been doing what Newfoundlands, as guardians and comforters, are bred to do. I got down on my knees and begged her to forgive me. She ran right up, put her paws on my shoulders, and, wagging her tail, licked my face and the face of the injured kitten. That was the first of many times that Nanny's compassion and forgiveness would prove greater than my own.

A Subject
Not Worth Considering

Carol and I were walking thirsty along a beach at Isla de
Mujeres in the Yucatán. Up amidst the palm trees we saw a thatched
enclosure with a soft drink cooler at the back. Hurrying toward it, we
came upon the proprietor — a bespectacled little potbellied man wearing only a pair of Jockey shorts. He was weaving a hammock with such
absorption that he didn't seem to notice us. The hammock was strung
between two of the *palapa's* support poles. Several other hammocks,
all of them of the Caribbean sea colors that surround the island —
hammocks far more beautiful than any I had seen before — were laid
out on a row of tin chairs. He paid no attention while we picked up the
hammocks, opened and spread them, oohing and aahing at their
beauty. As he flicked the shuttle from hand to hand through the twisted
strands of turquoise and blue thread, a fish seemed to be skimming
back and forth through the waves. Apparently he wasn't going to ac-
knowledge our presence of his own accord, so I finally interrupted to

ask if we could buy a couple of Cokes. He waved a finger toward the cooler, indicating that we should take our drinks and put our money in a coin box. After we had sat there awhile drinking and watching, we asked whether the hammocks were for sale. He looked up with exasperation. No, he told us, these were just gifts he wove to give to his friends. Except for selling the *refrescos,* he made his living working in the kitchen of the hotel out there at the end of the sandspit. There was always a lot of argument on the job, and conflict at home too. But when he was weaving – except when somebody like us insisted on interrupting – he entered a state of no thought. Nothing whatsoever entered his mind. He was totally happy. It was only to be in total happiness for a time that he wove hammocks. "That's amazing," I said. "Have you ever heard of the Buddha? The Buddha said something very similar." The weaver shrugged. "That's good. I don't mind what the Buddha says. He can say what he likes." Carol said, "What about Gandhi? You even look like Mahatma Gandhi." The weaver looked down at himself, hoisted his shorts up. "I suppose so. I don't know. Yes, I've heard of the man." I said, "Do you realize that people like Gandhi and the Buddha struggled for years to achieve no-thought? Many of the saints considered the state you arrive at through your weaving to be the long-sought goal of supreme enlightenment." The man looked at us over his glasses. "Maybe," he said with a shrug, and got back to work.

Tempting the Devil

On the fifth day of a water fast, I put on a white linen suit to match my spiritually elegant mood and set forth across the field beyond the San Miguel riding school to the canyon where, hidden away some thirty feet below the rim, was a cave I often climbed down to when I wanted to meditate. Having again managed the perilous descent, I sat myself on the hard ground at the very edge of the cave, folded my legs into the lotus position, and surveyed the beauty before me. The cacti that had found purchase on the opposite wall of the canyon were flowering; birds were singing. I felt God's presence so strongly that I said out loud, "I could meet the devil right now, and he could do me no harm." No sooner had I spoken these words than, sure enough, I heard a scrabbling on the rocks above. With a bound, there he stood beside me: the ugliest, surliest human being I had ever seen. It would have been comical, he was such a caricature of the devil himself, had I not realized that I was in serious trouble. His clothes were soiled and ripped, his hair grimed with dirt and grease. He had a scar on his cheek; his whole face was pocked with blackheads. He asked what a fancy-dressed "caballero" like me was doing here, and sat down next to me. I said, "Nothing." "Very dangerous," he said. Swiftly his hand was against my lower back. "Someone could take your money and push you over the cliff." I laughed. "No," I said, "The people around here are very good people. Nobody would ever do such a thing to me." "*Si señor*," he insisted. "Someone big like me could come and kill you so easy right now." His hand pushed on my back. "No, no," I said, "I'm not in the least worried." I was struggling inside not to let terror get the best of me. I looked at him directly, with all the love I could muster. He showed me his rotten teeth, removed the hand from my back, clenched the fist, and started reaming it with the finger of his other hand. "You want to . . . ?" "*Muchas gracias*," I said, "But, you see, I am one of those who prefers women." He said, "If a person came down here and wanted to fuck you and you wouldn't fuck him, this person could push you off this cliff right now." "Oh, no, hombre. Such a person would not do such a thing." We played this game for another half hour, before he jumped up and was gone. I envisioned him walking along the cliff above me, stopping, wondering what had possessed him not to rob this obviously rich gringo, fuck him in the ass, and push him over the edge. I could see him change his mind, turn. I got out of the lotus and tried to stand up. My legs had gone dead. I scrambled on my knees up the rocks. When I reached the top, there he was hurrying toward me. Legs still tingling, I nevertheless managed to run away. This event remains a puzzling theological event. How can you manifest a devil you don't even believe in? Was this God's way of mocking my spiritual vanity? It was enough to make a fundamentalist out of me.

A Silly Goose

During the concert reading at a church social hall of a play by Pinter, two characters were seated on stools about six feet apart: an old and a young man. As director, I was standing backstage watching some three hundred mostly white-haired ladies through a crack in the curtain to see whether the play would be too avant-garde for their tastes. It was puzzling. Half of the women weren't looking at the stage at all. They kept staring into their laps with stern expressions. For them the play was clearly a flop, a disaster. But the other women were doing just the opposite. They were sitting up straight, wide-eyed and fascinated by Harold, who was playing the young man. Even when the old man was speaking, their eyes stayed fixed upon Harold. The mystery cleared up at the end of the first act when Harold's girlfriend appeared backstage in a tizzy. Thanks to his ridiculous scorn for the inhibitions of underwear, she said, it had finally happened: One of his testicles had fallen through a rip in his pants. It had bobbed very nicely up and down in the spotlight, thank you, while he sat there facing the audience spread-legged like some innocent boob. When Harold was delivering his lines, she said, he got so tense that, sure, his testicle climbed into hiding. But during the old man's speeches it would relax and descend again. "Like a yo-yo," she said as she slipped off her yellow silk panties. "Wear these," she said, "you silly goose." And he did. But the hole was still in his pants. A better solution would have been to find a safety pin. Had it not been for the panties, Harold would not have become known about town as the goose that laid the golden egg.

When a Gringo
Tells a Lie

I was hiking along the Rio Laja with my Newfoundland dog
Nanny when a campesino burst out of a cornfield and strode toward me
shouting, "Make me a gift of your dog." I said I was sorry but the dog
was my best friend. He set his fists on his hips and laughed. "Don't you
have any human friends that you need a dog for a friend? A dog is not
for friendship. A dog is for work. What work does this dog do?" I said,
"We take walks in the country together." He said, "Yes, I've seen you.
You throw sticks in the river and she jumps in and brings them back.
Give her to me. My dog doesn't serve me for nothing. Yours will. She
will herd my cattle and guard my house and my children, and I can
teach her to do many other important things. What good is jumping in
the river after a stick?" I said, "She was originally bred to rescue sailors
who fall off of ships on the high seas. I'm keeping her in training." "Ah,
bueno, she's a rescuer then. And you're training her to save people who
fall in the water." "That's right. People, animals, any living thing that

falls in the water, she will rescue." "That's good, *señor.*" He stuck his fingers in his mouth and gave a whistle. A skinny dog came sidling up to him out of the corn, tail between its legs. He picked it up, carried it to the river and threw it in. The dog went down, came up, struggled against the current, went under again. "Nanny!" I shouted. "Go get him!" But she just stood there. So I picked up a stick and threw it next to the drowning dog's head. Nanny sprang into the water with a big splash, paddled out, and retrieved the stick right next to where the dog was frantically struggling. Three times Nanny retrieved the stick, ignoring the dog. The campesino spat on the ground. He returned to his cornfield. I kicked off my huarches, rolled up my pant legs, and was about to wade into the river when a woman who was washing clothes on the bank upstream leaped up and ran toward me. "Stop, gringo! That dog is my husband's. My husband can do what he pleases with him. You have no right to go save him." "But your husband is going to let the dog drown," I said. She waggled her finger at me. "No, gringo. If you had told my husband the truth, that dog would not be drowning. You are the drowner of that dog. If you and not your dog go into the water to pull him out, my husband will feel like a fool for believing you. He will be very insulted, and will put a stop to you with his machete. Truly, I am telling you the truth." Nanny and I watched the dog get carried downstream. After the dog had vanished around a bend, the campesino appeared again carrying an armload of freshly picked corn. He dropped six ears at my feet. "Go ahead and pick them up," he said. "They are the best in my field. Three I give to you as a gift. Three are for that useless, *pinche* dog of yours."

Not One Centavo

It's a shock for a saunterer to return to the United States. Except for the state and national parks, there's hardly anywhere in the countryside a person can walk. The fields are all fenced in, the woods posted with warning signs. Even the roads are frightening what with attack dogs rushing at you, and men in pickups passing with gun racks in the back window. In Mexico, you'll rarely find any of this. I spent years going to the market, buying cheese, a roll, and some fruit for my shoulder bag, getting on a third-class bus with its altar to the Virgin, its amiable peasants, curious children and animals. I'd ask the driver to let me off anywhere I pleased along the road, and I'd hike cross-country. No fences except to keep the cattle in; herders who doffed their sombreros and greeted me with the true "A-Dios," urging me to go with God. I'd walk through dusty villages with their church doors always open, everything peaceable. I'd sit on a ridge or by a river and nobody bothered me except to stop for a friendly chat. If it rained, I found shelter in one of the shepherd chapels that dot the hills. I got held up only once. Two guys jumped me way out in the country. They said they regretted it very much, but they had taken a vow to kill a gringo after what had been done to a friend of theirs while they were wetbacks in Texas. I told them I understood. I had seen what happens to Mexicans in the United States. Thank God it wasn't that way for gringos here. While one of them held a knife at my back, the other walked along beside me. We talked of everyday things. Then I told how it was revealed to me by a voice that I should move to Mexico just after I survived a swim across the Golden Gate. I said how much I loved walking like this through the Mexican countryside. "Everybody's like you," I said. "So friendly." "We're going to kill you," the one behind me said. I said there were some guys in California who were going to kill me once, but they weren't friendly at all. The guy beside me said I was right; there was nothing friendly about the *Norte Americanos.* He told about swimming the Rio Grande, all the harrowing experiences on the other side. Up ahead, I saw a trench in the earth and knew that this is where they planned to kill me. They stopped me there, pushed me back and forth, took my shoulder bag and wallet. I raised my hands. "Wait," I said, "Before you start, couldn't you just give me back five pesos." They got surly and demanded to know what use five pesos would be for me when I was dead. "The thing is," I said, "I might survive. I might be able to crawl as far as the highway. Can't you give me back enough for bus fare, just in case?" "Not one centavo!" the one in front of me said. "*Ni un centavo* will we give you, gringo," said the other. "Now go away from here and never come back!" "Not even a single centavo?" I said, my eyes watering. They gave me a shove. I walked away. I never looked over my shoulder.

A Little Nap

My brother Roland and I phoned my father in Santa Barbara. We told him we wanted to come visit. We were both longing to have the proverbial father-son talk we had put off all these years; the one where he would finally tell us the story of his life. He said, "I'm only sixty-eight. I'll tell you the story of my life when I'm an old man. Don't rush me." I suppose Dad thought we wanted him to reveal things he'd tried to hide. We went to visit him anyway. He took us right out to the tennis courts to show that he could still beat us. But he and my stepmother, Ginette, lost to me and Roland. That evening Ginette complained that my father was always rushing off to his labs; she felt abandoned. Dad misunderstood this as an affront to his virility. Embarrassed in front of his boys, he tried the next day to prove his prowess, but again he was on the losing side, this time with me. He did not lose graciously. I challenged my brother to singles. He had just lost a promotion at his university because of an anti-Vietnam War group he'd founded called the Up-Against-the-Wall-Mother-Fuckers in honor of the cop who had harassed them. Add to that the tension my brother suffered since childhood every time Dad had a tantrum on the court and it only took two double faults for Roland to have a tantrum of his own. He smashed his racket on the ground and marched into the nearby woods. "But what's going on?" Dad said. That night, Ginette went to bed early saying pointedly that she wanted to finish an article about men who neglect their wives. "*La merde!*" Dad shouted. "I'm about to make a major breakthrough!" "But you have to take a little *nap* once in a while," she cried. In the morning, Dad gave us a tour of the labs where he was re-creating dolphin sounds on his speech synthesis machine. "My machine is talking to the dolphins and the dolphins are talking to my machine. But I don't yet know what they're saying. When I find out, I'll win the Nobel Prize." We drove to the courts. Again, Dad was on the losing side. My brother, in another funk, walked off into the woods. Ginette had gone to fix lunch. Dad wanted to play singles. He proceeded to chase every shot like a maniac. I tried to ease up. He accused me of giving him points, insisted we play them over, no mercy. When Ginette returned, the set was at 22–22. She begged us to stop, but Dad refused. So I hit some shots long on purpose, and lost. Walking shakily off the court, he laughed and shook his head at me almost pityingly. "So that's what it's come to. You think you have to let me win." My brother returned. We all got in the car. Dad's head fell over the wheel. Ginette took hold of his shoulders. She looked back at us, said, "*Mon Dieu,* he's dying." Dad raised up, said pleasantly, "Yes, what's wrong with that?" and collapsed again. We pulled him out of the car and lay him on the ground. He died with the same smile I used to see on his face when he was taking a little nap.

I Serve to Exacerbate
a Lovers' Quarrel

Anice-looking young guy who had been eyeing me for some time at a lunch counter in San Francisco moved over next to me. He asked if I was waiting for somebody. I said, "Yes. I'm writing a script that involves the Hopi Indians. A man who knew the Hopi well was going to meet me here half an hour ago and tell me what he knew about them. I guess he's not coming." "Relax," the guy said, "I can tell you about the Hopi. Can I ever! I had a Hopi Indian lover for two years. He revealed tribal secrets to me that most people have no notion of. What say we have dinner tonight? On me. Bring your notebook." I met him at five as he came out from work at Macy's. He was already dressed much more elegantly than I was, but he said he looked tacky and insisted we go first to his apartment so he could change. On his walls were ass shots of nude men. I told myself I had no problem with that. He got dressed in this Edwardian kind of costume complete with coat, tails, top hat, and off we strode to what had been an Italian family restaurant when

I'd known it. Now it was a posh gay restaurant/bar with Tiffany chandeliers. Lined up at the brass rail were the handsomest men I have ever seen – not effeminate at all. Every one of them looked like a movie star; they were all dressed in the Edwardian style. The Hopi's ex-lover and I sat at a table. All eyes checked us out. "Let's order drinks for now," the guy said. "We can eat later." We sipped at margaritas and made small talk. I tried to get him into the subject of the Hopi, but he kept stalling. Suddenly a silence fell over everyone. Pushing through the swinging doors from the vestibule appeared an incredibly handsome Clark Gable-looking dude. All eyes turned on him. Haughtily, he surveyed the scene. The Hopi-lover seized my hand, leaned toward me, gazed into my eyes, said ardently, "Pierre, oh my Pierre, I love you so much." Before I could pull my hand away, the new arrival's head had snapped around; he'd seen us; he'd heard. He glowered. He spun on his heel and strode out. The Hopi-lover dropped my hand. He said coldly: "I don't need you anymore, Pierre, so why don't you just leave." I promptly did so. Out on Grant Avenue without my supper, I was pissed off. Yet I couldn't help but admire his ingenuity.

The Golden Door

Scott led me down the basement stairs of an apartment building on Russian Hill. We walked along a corridor to a mildewy room where some cadaverous-looking people of retirement age in suits and gowns were seated on tin chairs eagerly looking toward a candlelit table adorned with a cross, a Star of David, images of Jesus, Buddha, Mohammed, plaques for the Order of the Eastern Star, Elks, Lions, Kiwanis Club, Virgin Mary. We sat on a bench along one wall next to three longhair, stoned-out hippie types in *Yellow Submarine*-style rock-and-roll clothing that reeked of marijuana. According to Scott, they came here as devotedly as the others. When the woman Scott had told me so much about entered, I was surprised, expecting someone more mystical-looking. This woman was your typical plump, blue-haired frumpy clubwoman in a gingham dress, bubbling with good cheer as she greeted us in downhome style: "Glad to see y'all, real good havin' ya here. Let's get right on down to business." All hands shot up.

She called on a man who asked whether he should buy a piece of real estate. She closed her eyes for a moment, opened them wide. "Why honey," she said, "my little spirit guide tells me it would be a great idea to buy right now, yes, absolutely. Next." For an hour she answered questions about whether or not to buy, sell, invest, what jobs to apply for, what new ventures to start: a boring, thoroughly materialistic medium, it seemed, until she got to one of the hippie's questions: "Dr. Rousseau, can I pass through the golden door?" "Why, honey, you can if you trust in Mrs. Rousseau. If you believe in me, yes, you can pass right through the golden door into the spirit world and come back any time you please. Didn't I tell you you'd find a drummer for your band? And didn't you find him the very next day? Didn't I say you should do that concert in Chicago, and didn't it lead like I said to your cutting a record deal? Well then honey, sure, you go right on through that golden door." "Thank you, Mrs. Rousseau!" cried the elated musician. "You're welcome, child. Now y'all be good and trust in me until we meet again, hear?" The next morning I was seated in my cab in front of the Sir Francis Drake reading the *Chronicle* when I saw on the front page an article headlined "Youth Leaps Through Golden Door, Survives." It told of how this same disciple of Mrs. Rousseau had jumped from the center span of the Golden Gate Bridge, the first ever not to be killed from that height. He had been pulled out of the water with nothing but a bruised heel; said he had passed through the Golden Door, enjoyed a visit with friends on the other side, and had returned to this world feeling just great. "A far-out experience," he'd said. The article ended with a disclaimer by Mrs. Rousseau, saying that her "golden door" was a metaphor for spiritual passage. She begged her disciples please never again to take it literally.

As Good a Place
as Any

Back in San Miguel, broke, I heard that Ravi Shankar would be performing with his group at the Palacio de Bellas Artes in Mexico City. Hearing him live was one of my dreams. With guidance from a friend who played the sitar, I had just reached that thrilling point where I could actually follow the entire progression of one of the ragas. I sold my Mayan flute, paid what to me was a fortune for a ticket, and took the four-hour bus ride. I didn't have enough money left for a good hotel, so I hiked from the metro to my hotel-of-last-resort, El Gran Hotel Texas. I got to my room at about three, hung my clothes on the chair, took a trickling shower, and lay down on the bed, my head raised up on a hard pillow. The room was painted a pale green and smelled of toilet disinfectant. A shade had been pulled down permanently over the window, but there was a rip in it revealing a blackened brick wall. I could hear the traffic honking, the voices of street vendors. The cracked paint on the ceiling was peeled back here and there to expose clouds of crumbling plaster. I lay there thinking of this and that. For some reason, I began to feel enormously contented, with nothing to do until seventhirty, when I would take the stroll down through the park to the Palacio. I even enjoyed the alternating waves of sorrow and bliss that occasionally coursed through my body, as they always do when I am reduced to lying on a bed in a very cheap hotel room in a foreign city with not enough money left to go out to a good restaurant. Hours passed. I stopped thinking about anything in particular, relaxed into a wonderful doldrum where the alternation between rejoicing in life and feeling sorry for myself ceased altogether. Though at some point I knew it must be time to go to the concert, I could summon no urge to rise to the occasion. Not even these many years of wanting to hear Ravi Shankar could motivate me to get up from where I lay so entirely at peace inside myself. Why deny this peacefulness? Why abandon immediate happiness for even the most extravagant promise of happiness to come? It would seem a betrayal of the present moment, its obscure, far-fromeveryone, anonymous calmness – calmness at the other extreme from the crescendos Shankar would surely concoct until musicians and audience had surfaced onto peaks of mirthful hysteria. I stayed there in the seedy little hotel room all evening long and through the night, and have never regretted not seeing Shankar. When I hear him on tape, he always transports me back to that smelly little room. I can taste the melancholy Mexico City grit between my teeth, smell the astringent quietness of being there where no friend knows I am, in as good a place as any, with nothing that matters anymore, however wonderful or terrible, however wild the music of the world around me.

The Buddha
Saves My Life

Arich shipbuilder whom my partner Carol had fallen in love
with invited us to visit him and his wife in Paris for a few weeks, all ex-
penses paid. Afterward, we would spend a few months at their estate in
Mallorca, then board the *Cosmos*, a new sailing ship he was outfitting
for a journey to explore the life of dolphins. My father's former protégé
in the study of dolphin language had agreed to head the scientific team
if I went along. I would write about our adventure. Stanley and Helga
would then build us a house in the orchard behind theirs so that I could
become the tutor of their children. I said thanks, but no. Carol was flab-
bergasted. Stanley had just offered me my dream. But I didn't especially like him. Maybe I was jealous. In any case, it would have been
hypocritical to go. I said aloofly that I had decided long ago never to
return to France as a mere tourist, but only when I had achieved such
acclaim as a writer that I could legitimately hobnob with the Paris lite-
rati. At such a time, I would go with my children, and I would show

them the village where I was raised as a boy. Understandably, Carol couldn't wait that long. She went on her own while I holed up miserably in a pad in San Francisco's Chinatown. To rub salt in the wound, she sent a card rejoicing that, by chance, she had come upon my daughter Michele sitting on a park bench beside the Seine during a break from her studies in England. Carol, Stanley, and Michele (Helga had gone home) were off for a visit to my boyhood territory. They'd write me all about it. I was devastated. Surely Stanley knew how badly all this was hurting me – how insulted I felt; defeated; robbed of my loves, of my destiny. I walked the streets consumed by hatred. Back in my room, I decided to kill myself. I sat on the floor to say a prayer before taking the walk to the Golden Gate Bridge. As was my habit, I decided to end my prayer with a reading from a sacred text. The day before at City Lights I had picked up a copy of the Dhammapada, the earliest recorded sermons of the Buddha. I opened the book at random and saw the exact words I had been muttering to myself for days: "He hurt me, he insulted me, he defeated me, he robbed me." The text went on to say that "those who think such thoughts will not be free from hate . . . but those who think not such thoughts will be free from hate, for hate is not conquered by hate, hate is conquered by love." My hate for Stanley miraculously fell away. I saw that, out of pride, I had refused his offering of love. If Carol had fallen so madly in love with him, well . . . he was a very lovable person. I surrendered my attachment to Carol, my imagined destiny, the possessiveness I felt toward my daughter. I went out on the streets, thrilled with the world again, amazed at the Buddha for having known how to enter my room in Chinatown, after a 2,500-year journey through space and time, so as to reach me just as I was about to close the book on life.

Chac-Mol

I spent an evening atop the temple Kukulkan at Chichén Itzá. Underneath me slept one of the stone gods, Chac-Mol. By moonlight I watched currents of energy streaming from one temple to another. Behind me was the observatory where by night priests had watched the movement of the stars and by day the movements made by the shadow-stones, which would tell them when to abandon the temples to the Toltecs who wanted their hearts. I could imagine how, down there in the courtyard, the priests must have walked very slowly, perhaps inching along under the enormous headdresses. I thought of how I had escaped a culture of friends dying on speed to come to this ruin where the Mayans had worshipped the slowest form of life we can commune with – the life of stone. In the morning, I asked Carol to lead me across the courtyard while I closed my eyes and let myself be pulled by currents I could feel flowing under my foot through the grass. She walked me a long way, then stopped me and told me to reach out. My fingers, exploring rough stone, recognized – by the drawn-up knees, the bowl on the belly, body resting on elbows, head turned sideways – that this was a Chac-Mol. I sat down in front of him. Eyes still closed, I got into his same posture. Turning my head until Carol said that I was looking exactly where he was, I opened my eyes and saw far across the court-yard at the top of the Temple of a Thousand Columns, also resting on his elbows, another Chac-Mol looking directly down at me. A powerful mental current began to circulate between us. I told him how Carol yesterday had pretended to be a priest walking toward me between the columns to plunge a knife in my heart, and I'd understood that she had hurried over here from Mallorca to let me know that she was sacrificing the love she felt for me to the stronger pull of a man who was my op-posite – a man of speed.

Chac-Mol said that my people would have come to know the soul of the temple stones if only we had paid attention to what he and his fel-low Chac-Mols were looking at before moving them around. As for the sacrificial well, it was a wonderful swimming hole for him and his brothers. I laughed and told him about going swimming with my own brother when we were boys; about me and Roland lying on our elbows like this in front of the sumac huts we built on opposite hills, staring at each other as we practiced telepathy. Chac-Mol said, "Go back to the farm. Talk to your brother. Offer up a sacrifice. Then seek out the soul of the stone." The words seemed so melodramatic that I would dismiss them as hallucination until the next year when I *would* go to the farm, and my brother would tell me about the teacher of his two boys. Her name, he said, was Nancy Ortenstone. Ortenstone, meaning "soul of the stone." I was afraid to become involved with a woman who had chil-dren, so I didn't let him introduce me to her. But she would rise from a bench at a party one night and dance with me, and it wouldn't be until after I had fallen in love with her that I'd find out she was this same woman. And we would drive to the farm, throw water on the hot stones of my grandfather's sauna; we would purge ourselves of pain and begin a wondrous new life together. I knew none of this at Chichén Itzá, ex-cept that a sacrifice had to be made first, and then the stone god would fulfill his promise.

The Golden Ring

Wherever my Uncle André and Tante Yvonne went, they created gatherings of happy people. They always lived in one old country house or another where they held feasts, soirées, took long walks through the woods and fields with the dog pack leading the way, the adults telling stories, philosophizing, extemporizing poems and the children marching along, happily bringing up the rear. From the time we arrived at their place to the time we left, my brother and I were deliriously happy. Even my parents managed to joke and laugh, play games, and get along wonderfully . . . until we drove home and the arguments resumed. André had hung out in Paris with the surrealists; he had the true bohemian spirit and was my role model. After he died at age 49, my aunt divided up his belongings, sending me a number of his books signed by authors who had now become famous. She also sent a box of his clothes, which I put on one night – trousers, belt, shirt, tweed jacket, and scarf. I walked around San Francisco engaging people in his kind of merry-eyed questioning. After my aunt joined a Swiss order of Protestant artist-nuns, she hitchhiked cross-country in her self-styled nun's habit to come visit me. Her presence was pure radiant light and love. While we were at a cabin in the Sierras, I heard her one night enter my room and kneel by my bed. I was about to seize her in my arms and do something foolish when I realized that she was praying for me. In the morning, fighting my infatuation, I went swimming with her in a mountain river. Suddenly she gave a cry. Her wedding ring had slipped off her finger. I dove and dove, but couldn't find it. Finally I had to drive her to her bus. But I returned, dove for two more days, stirring up sand in the pool where we had swum, until I found it and was able to mail it back—but not before I had put on my uncle's jacket and taken a long walk, holding the ring while I wed myself to my aunt and uncle's view of life as continuous wonder and celebration. I hauled my uncle's books around for years, dreaming of some day belonging to a bohemian circle like the one he had so enjoyed in Paris and re-created in the United States. In Mexico, when I reduced my belongings to what I could fit in a backpack, I put the books up for sale. A searcher for rare books came over to check things out. When he saw the books signed by Breton, Dali, Cocteau, and the others, his eyes bugged out. He bought them all for a few pesos and thought he'd gotten away with an incredible steal. I watched him pack the books into a gunnysack. Sweating with excitement, he lugged them to his car. The sight of him making off with the books of these gifted men, not because he loved to read, but because he thought he was going to make a big profit on them was wonderfully pathetic. The spirits of my uncle and aunt sat down on the ground with me and laughed for all of us.

A Rosary of Faces

Carol left me. I got very sick. I think I wanted to die. People from the poor neighborhood I was living in knew I couldn't get out of bed, so they snuck in and stole almost all my stuff. My friends were shunning me. When I got halfway well, I packed a small bag, abandoned the rest, and took a bus, any bus. I ended up in San Luis Potosí, a religious city. Every day I went to the cathedral to pray. The priest and congregation kept incanting the same words like a mantra. Their words seemed to rise up over the candle-lit walls and cascade upon us. I finally translated the words to mean, "The kingdom of heaven is within you." Remembering the way the women said their rosaries, I went back to my room and, sitting in meditation, brought before my third eye, one by one, the faces of every person I could think of, living or dead. Keeping a regular rhythm so that no one face would be lingered on or quickly passed over to be loved more or less than another, I summoned each face in its most radiant expression, as it might appear while welcoming a loved one back from a long journey. To each face I said, "The kingdom of heaven is within you," and found myself smiling more and more happily as they lit up in response. Eager to find other faces to love, I went out on the streets. For days I walked, looking into faces in the passing crowd while saying to myself, "The kingdom of heaven is within you." The face that literally transformed my in-sight was that of a grouchy, hunched over butcher in a bloody apron, with a slab of meat slung over his shoulder. For an instant, his eyes twinkled, and I saw God peeking out at me. From then on, every face I looked into flashed me this same glance of mirth, revealing the divinity so cunningly stowed away, yet delighted at being found out, relieved that I had finally caught on to the game: good, bad, ugly or beautiful, whatever our mood at the time—their conspiratorial faces said—we all wear the masks of God. I walked in bliss for weeks saying my rosary of faces, first in Mexico, then in the United States. When I got to St. Paul, I applied for a job that I was much less qualified for than the many other applicants. I was still saying silently "The kingdom of heaven is within you" as I looked into the eyes of each of the ten staff members who sat in a circle interviewing me. They started laughing, these gods and godesses, delighted that I knew them for their secret selves. They hired me and showered me with love while I was there. Eventually I stopped seeing the divinity in their eyes. They became human again, with all their foibles. I have asked myself why I so seldom resume the "kingdom of heaven" walks and visualizations when they bring me such bliss. Perhaps God prefers not to show his or her presence in the eyes of others except in times of crisis when we're desperately in need of realizing who we truly are. Otherwise, the Creator seems content to stay hidden within appearances.

Howling with the Moon

S till suffering from the breakup with Carol, I retired to a cottage my grandfather had built eighty years ago on a spring-fed lake in the north woods of Wisconsin far from anybody. There were eighty acres of field and woodland to wander on. The best times were at night, walking naked under the moon and stars, my fear gradually diminishing, then gone; my eyes growing accustomed to the dark until I could see the wild animals who moved past without paying much attention to me. I realized that many creatures who used to come into the open during the day had been forced by hunters to become night creatures now. Deer, bear, fox, woodchuck, skunk, porcupine, mink – none seemed concerned about me at night even when I stayed in darkness against a tree and watched them browse or romp close by. Night was their time of safety and celebration. They scampered about in play. It made me feel wistful sometimes to think of how they hid their joy from humans. For three days in a row, as I was seated on my blanket in a lotus position after doing yoga at the water's edge, a weasel came out from his log and sprawled out next to me. He stayed there until my legs grew numb and I had to move. Across the lake was a virgin forest I had never dared enter as a boy, for old man Frankenthal would not tolerate trespassers. But at night, aged forty-five, while the loons laughed, I finally dared make the half-mile swim across the lake, climbing over logs onto the mossy banks and groping my way amidst the trees. Or I would climb the hill where three generations of our family had once made hay while they laughed and joked. My grandparents had lugged rocks against their bellies to a mound at the center of the field when they cleared it. This mound was their true burial mound to me, and it became my temple. I loved to play my recorder (my wooden flute) up there. Its high sound on windless nights expanded in a circle until the dogs on the farms far off in all directions starting barking. I could picture the farmers climbing out of bed and grabbing their shotguns to see if a fox was in the chicken coop. The barking aroused dogs on farms farther and farther outward until the circumference of their barking reached the village of Phelps seven miles away. I couldn't hear the town dogs, but I knew they had started up. I liked to think that the playing of my flute would eventually cause the barking to expand outward across the entire United States and, who knows, perhaps up to the Dog Star itself. Having no sexual partner, I found myself being aroused by the full moon. One night, seated on the shore near the cottage, I saw a woman in the moon. The reflections of her voluptuous white fullness spread and shimmered so urgently toward me across the soft approaching waves that, with my hands planted on two voluptuous rocks behind me, I had a spontaneous orgasm while leaning back howling.

Banshee

I had seen her almost every afternoon when I was a baby left alone in my crib: the head of a long-haired malicious old woman circling the ceiling, glaring down at me. My parents didn't believe me when I told them about her. The only way I could get rid of her was to roll over onto my stomach, shut my eyes tight, and pound her out of my head. I was a congenital head pounder. In the middle of the night I would be startled awake by a hand clutching at the neck of my pajamas, shaking me. My father would scream at me to shut up and quit pounding my head. I pleaded with him, cried that I didn't know what I'd been doing. He must have taken it for some kind of masturbation. He resorted to regular spankings. I tried not to pound my head. But once the hag appeared, there was no other way to get rid of her; so I had to. I struggled not to fall asleep before her image was knocked out of my mind, but I'd pass out, and then, bam! bam! bam! I'd be startled awake by Dad's hand pounding away at my backside while he screamed that I was keeping the whole house awake. He tried everything to stop me. Despite Mom's protests, he even put a brick in my pillow, but the hag, the head pounding, and the punishments continued until we left that house in Detroit when I was eleven. Who was she? I only found out thirty years later while house-sitting for a friend. I'm seated at dusk on a patio at the edge of a golf course in Borrego Springs, California. The ground rocks under me. I watch a wave roll across the golf course as if someone had picked up a blanket and shaken it. I check out the house. Nothing broken, but the electricity out. On a battery radio, I get the news that I was sitting right on the epicenter of a small earthquake. I find a candle and candleholder. That night I run my fingers along the bookshelf, pull out a slim leather-bound volume, and settle into the easy chair. The book is by Lady Wilde, entitled *Irish Legends and Folk Tales*. I open at random to a chapter entitled "Banshees" and read words something like this: *Banshee: the head of an old hag with malicious intent usually seen circling around the ceiling of a room.* She exists! What an incredible relief! I'm not alone. I belong to a whole nation of people who have seen this archetype. But why Irish? Even as I'm wondering this, my daughter is off touring Ireland with the man who will become her husband. Though neither she nor he have any Irish descendants I know of, they will go on to form a band that plays Irish traditional music. They will perform at weddings, dances, at Irish pubs; cut a few records; eventually name their group after my book *Walking on Air*. My daughter's accent will even come to sound a bit Irish. After all, our Norman ancestors were Celts. Do we carry the same creatures of folklore and legend in our DNA? Am I someday going to meet one of the little people? I hope so.

The Head
in the Fire

I arrived at the MacDowell Colony in New Hampshire one October afternoon with everything I owned loaded into my truck. A typically taciturn New England farmer-type escorted me and left me without a word at my assigned cottage, a chapellike building hidden away in the woods, equipped with both central heating and a stack of logs for the fireplace. Above the mantel I found inscribed the names of such intimidating ex-tenants as . . . were they e.e. cummings, Leonard Berstein, Clifford Odets? Anyhow, such artists as I felt I must at least try to live up to. Right away I put my typewriter on a table facing the breathtaking fall colors of the hills. Trying not to gaze out, I got to work staring at a sheet of blank paper instead. I did this every day for two months and was never able to write a word. At noon a silent joop would pull up, and someone – I never once heard or saw him – would leave on my porch a basket filled with wonderful lunch goodies. At dusk, I would hike to the mansion where a Swiss cook served some thirty of us writers, painters, and composers with delicious dinners. The wine loosened our tongues. Our talk always seemed to concern agents, royalties, advances, the recent scandals, entrée into other art colonies, connections to universities, but especially the latest on the clandestine and opportunistic sexual encounters in which I was taking part with such self-loathing. Few of us talked about our artistic vision or our work per se, and I suspected that I was not the only one having difficulty producing any, given such "perfect" conditions. I left our conversations each time with greater self-loathing for having failed to remember my artistic ideal, playing blasé by pandering to our common greed, lust, and ambition. Near the end, I stayed away from the others for three days of yoga and fasting. Then I built a huge bonfire. After the fire had calmed to a glow, I took everything I had ever kept of my unpublished writing – five novels, numerous stories and poems. I stacked them up and set them on the fire. Very soon, the flames licking around the edges rounded the stack to form the shape and size of my own head. With fascination, I watched a mouth and two eyes, perfectly placed, break out in blue flame. Pages at the top curled back, as from my brain, so that I could read a few words or phrases before flames rolled them back and charred them. I left MacDowell Colony having unwritten my entire life. In that happily burned-out state, I returned me from the gravity of a "serious writer" to the levity of one who loves his art again. I have never regretted burning those manuscripts, much as I sometimes wonder how good they were. I felt that I had made a sacrifice to my own conscience. Instinct had correctly told me that any powerful act of creation must be preceded by an equally powerful act of destruction.

I Become
a Happiness Gorilla

At a gathering of poets in St. Paul, I saw a man and woman hugging each other and laughing on a couch in the candlelight. The happiness they exuded reminded me of my Uncle André and Tante Yvonne; and, as it turned out, like my aunt and uncle, they held weekly salons in the mansion they had reconstructed from a ruin on Ashland Avenue. Artists, intellectuals, bon-vivants gathered there. I never missed a Saturday night if I could help it; I could count on finding happiness at their house. My Finnish grandfather would easily have mistaken Alvaro Cardona-Hine for a lazy, no good, worthless dreamer. I never saw him working. He always seemed to be playing at something; cheerfully ready for any game. Yet he was and remains the most prolific and gifted artist I have ever known—painter, composer, poet, novelist, translator. He has obliterated the duality between work and play; and while I know that he has suffered as much or more than most of us, one would never guess it in his company. Joy is his element. And his wife, the poet and novelist Barbara McCauley, is the same way. To visit them was and is to receive a straight shot of happiness. Barbara and Alvaro have a gift for manifesting whatever we most yearn for, as if by magic. From a bench, at the first dance I attended at their house, rose a woman to dance with me, and Nancy and I have been together ever since, keeping alive that celebrative spirit that Alvaro and Barbara remind us (without having to say it) is our true moral duty. At one of their soirées I told about the night before when two people dressed as singing gorillas appeared at my nephew's birthday party, how it had been so wonderful to have a couple of happy apes burst into my life after so many strange and troubling ape encounters. Alvaro proposed that from now on we call each other "The Happiness Gorillas." We would include in our circle anyone who was willing to leave his or her problems behind and join our gatherings in the spirit of pure, uninterrupted happiness. Since then, I have never for a moment felt unhappy amidst the happiness gorillas. No matter what miseries or even outright tragedies have occurred in my life, I know that I can count on a new infusion of happiness each time I approach their golden circle. I was wishing they could all be with me one afternoon at the San Diego Zoo when I saw an incredible sight: a rare golden monkey sent as a goodwill gesture by the government of China. He was seated on a hill, almost as large as a gorilla, golden-haired, with a white face that was fixed in a thick, lipstick-red, outrageously happy smile. Yet I knew he must be miserable up there so alone on his prison hill. I cried out, "Greetings from the Happiness Gorillas." He fixed me with an intense gaze. For just a moment, all the hair on his body fanned out. He turned himself into a burst of blazing, golden sunshine – the most beautiful apparition I have ever seen. That smile fixed on his face came alive and was true; I felt it on my own mouth, and I knew that I had seen God in the ape at last. And though he remains in prison, I know that the release of him (or her) and all sentient beings into happiness is what our work and play on Earth is all about. We are not descended from the ape. We *are* the ape-god still seeking the creation's full measure of freedom and happiness.

The Wedding
of Fred and Matilda

While performing the wedding service, I would break into cold sweats; my heart would flutter, my legs tremble under my robe. I would hyperventilate so badly that I sometimes had to gasp, "Let us pause for a moment of silent prayer," until I regained enough breath to go on. Before a wedding, I lost whole nights of sleep worrying about it. Would I faint at the altar? Would my quaking hands be able even to hold on to the wedding book, let alone read the words? I decided it would be safer to memorize the service. But at a huge cathedral wedding I lapsed into the Gettysburg Address: "Dearly beloved, we are assembled here in the presence of God to join this man and this woman in holy wedded matrimony, which is instituted by God and made holy by all those who are truly great. Four score and seven years ago our fathers brought forth on this continent a new nation –" Though nobody seemed to notice my lapse, it made weddings hell for me from then on. Church weddings were the worst – waiting with the groom and best man in a dark room filled with our tension, walking out into an appalling hush, the sudden blast of the wedding march, seeing the usually dismayed parents, the bridesmaids struggling wide-eyed down the aisle on their shaky high heels, the bride and groom most often dazed or horrified. Sudden silence. My heart pounding as I shattered the life of innocence with my solemn words. To avoid church weddings, I'd suggest that we have a ceremony by the sea, in a garden, that we make it more of a true celebration. Ironically, this had made me the most popular marrying cleric in San Francisco. Protestants, Jews, atheists, even Buddhists insisted on being married by nobody but me. Determined not to have fear defeat me, I took on every request. I ended up doing weddings almost every day. For years after I left the ministry, when I heard the wedding march my eyes would blur, my body tremble. Perhaps I sensed that my own marriage would have a tragic ending. Perhaps, being only marginally Christian, I felt like a fraud. Anyhow, the terror of performing weddings ended when the little girl who became one of my daughters when I met my future wife Nancy asked if I would do the wedding service for Fred and Matilda, her two monkey dolls. I couldn't come up with an excuse, so I had to say yes, though even this monkey marriage made me fear a nervous breakdown, especially after the elaborate preparations. My other new daughter, Carla, held the tuxedoed Fred, while Jenny held Matilda, whose long gown their mother had worked on for days. The girls spoke the vows for the monkeys; helped them exchange rings. A teddy bear was best man. Nancy, serving as bridesmaid, looked at me reassuringly through the whole ceremony. I felt amazingly calm and happy. I couldn't believe how easily it went. When I pronounced Fred and Matilda man and wife, I knew that whatever had been wrong with me about marriage was ended and that Nancy and I would be together for the rest of our lives.

Synchronicity

Nancy and the girls trusted me when I asked them to join their lives to mine. Almost broke, we drove to Mexico. Though I'd burned everything I'd written, I'd guaranteed I would quickly write a book and sell it, something I hadn't managed to do since publishing my first book nine years before. I could not allow self-doubt to enter in for even a moment. But what would I write? A friend said to me, "Write about balance." Remembering that Abraham Maslow had called distractions the unacknowledged attractions whose energy can save us if we turn our window into a lens and let them pour into our point of focus, I stopped hiding behind my study door from the chaos in our lives, opened myself to it, and concentrated on restoring its balance. I read books about balance in physics, art, psychology; asked people in the plaza what they had to say about balance. I figured that if I kept harping on this one theme, synchronicity would begin to operate, just as Jung had said; the whole world, as Mann had promised, would start signaling. Sure enough, a mime sought me out to tell me about the difference between balancing on the slack and the tightrope. My friend Hiliry knocked on my door; she had joined a circus. She introduced me to Kimo the Clown, who taught me how to balance the comedy of happiness and sadness. I started to hang around the circuses that passed through town. Performers told me about their balancing techniques. While standing on my head doing yoga, I got the idea for a circus that loses its equilibrium when one of the acts – each representing a *chakra* – dies and can't be replaced. Synchronicity was now operating full blast. I chanced on an article by a psychiatrist about authors who treat their agents like father figures such that if the agent rejects their book they take it to be worthless, "even so far as to burn it." I fired my agent; the next day got a letter from my friend Marly Rusoff, who was entering the agenting business. Did I have a manuscript? I sent it, she sold it – but on condition I rewrite the climactic scene involving a mystical juggler. The reason the scene hadn't worked is that I'd failed to learn anything about the spiritual aspects of juggling. Now it was too late. My deadline was the next day. What to do? I remembered a story my grandmother told me about a monk who juggles before Our Lady, hurried to the cathedral, got on my knees before the Virgin, told her my problem. She smiled down as if to say, "I'll help you. Go write it." First I had to bid farewell to a friend who was leaving town. His door was answered by a stranger who said, "Hi, I'm Carlos. I hear you're writing a circus novel. I was a juggler in a circus for five years." He took me home; his whole family juggled for me. Carlos gave me a rare book on the mysticism of juggling. I wrote my revision, sent it off. *Walking on Air* was published. The check came when we were down to our last peso. Not being so frantically broke brought our lives back into balance.

Perpetual Wonder

The Bible says that love endures forever. On a cosmic scale, I don't doubt it. On the human scale, love seems to come and go. As far as I can see, the great constant appears to be wonder. Perhaps the universe itself is a vast expression of questions followed by answers that create within themselves new questions. Certainly we are always wondering about something. The beauty and reach of our questions determines the beauty and reach of our lives. My wife Nancy and I were both wondering how to get started on books we simply had to get written if we were going to survive in Mexico. Discussing what makes a good line in fiction, we observed that any sentence contains within it the germ of a question. We decided that if we simply wrote sentences that answered the most suspenseful question raised by the previous sentence while at the same time provoking another equally intriguing question in our answer, we could write books that were, in fact, a series of responses to the reader's ongoing sense of wonder. For an hour a day,

149

each of us would enter the other's study. The one who was writing the book would sit in an easy chair or lie on the couch while the other sat at the typewriter. After an initial statement was made – "Her name was Charlotte Helstrom," for example – the typist would ask a question: "Where was she living?"; and would type the other's answer: "She was living in a Saracen tower on the coast of Spain," and then ask another question: "What was she doing there?" "She was studying the mating habits of a rare waterbird who never laid her eggs until she had placed a small crystal in her nest." And so it went until both Nancy and I had finished the first drafts of our books entirely by answering questions. Of course the questions were never stated in the book, just the answers phrased as complete sentences. I doubt that anybody reading what we wrote would have deciphered our technique. Yet not only was the reader's wonder continually kept aroused and then satisfied, but the author was prevented from anticipating the direction of his or her story and thus becoming bored by it. If contradictions arose, the person taking down the answers was there to point this out. The rewrites allowed us to add, change, delete, and rearrange, or even to drop the original and start from scratch. Even if with other books we used the method only for a chapter or two, it was a wonderful way to get started. I recommend it not only to writers but to schoolteachers. If you think kids love asking questions, wait until you see how much they love *answering* questions as well.

An Abstract Enthusiast

In his late seventies, George Mayer became an abstract enthusiast. It no longer mattered what there was to enthuse about; anything would do. If we were watching the Giants play the Jets on the Mexican cable feed from the States, he might suddenly leap up and cry, "Touchdown!" I'd say, "No, George, he dropped the ball," and he'd cry, still dancing about, waving his arms, "Oh, my gosh, the Jets dropped it! Fantastic!" And I'd say, "The *Giants* dropped it," and he'd cry, "It was the *Giants!*" If he spotted me on the street, he could be counted on to start shouting some new fantastic piece of information. Hart Crane had been George's roommate in Greenwich Village before George met Dorothy, a magazine illustrator. He took her to the wilderness and began a long series of outdoor adventures. They were the rescue team at Glacier Point in Yosemite for thirty years. George would tie himself to a tree while he pushed the bonfire over the cliff during the famous "firefall." When he fell off the roof of the hotel at Glacier Point and broke his back, he and Dorothy returned permanently to Mexico. That summer, as if in grief, the hotel burned itself down. George was now a year-round, albeit increasingly senile spreader of enthusiasms at dances, hot-pool parties, even at bullfights where he cheered the bull and matador with equal ardor, much to the matador's dismay. Meanwhile, Dorothy seemed in decline. She, who was so quiet and clearheaded, must have found George's rantings hard to bear, especially while she was trying to paint. Always the gentleman, George realized that it was time to remove his enthusiasms to a more cosmic plane so that Dorothy could flourish. He yielded to cancer. We gathered around his sickbed for a laying on of hands. He was going fast. I came by one day. Dorothy said she'd been reading a terrific book about fabulous beasts who appeared at times of crisis. Just then, George cried out, "Dorothy! The bears!" We hurried to his bedside. He said the bears had come down from the hills and were surrounding his bed. Dorothy said, "Don't worry, George, they're just looking for garbage." He sat up, cried, "I'm not garbage!" The next day, we sent our daughter Jenny over to check on George. She found a huge dog pawing at the door. She knocked. It was hard for her and Dorothy to keep the dog from entering, but they did. During their struggle with the dog, George died. Dorothy underwent an imaginary illness, a real assault, and the destruction of her house, but she pulled herself out of it and went on to become the most radiant, inspiring person many of us have ever known. Now in her mid-nineties, she still writes the kind of mystical prose I can only aspire to, is an ever more marvelous painter, does yoga, holds Krishna Murti discussion groups, and has become the living expression of George's ongoing gift of being *en theos,* in God, the unconditional enthusiast eager to celebrate every aspect of the cosmos.

Nancy's Dream Bird
Saves Our Lives

A bird who had been conceived as a peripheral character in a novel Nancy was writing kept demanding her attention until she gave him an important role as friend and ally of the ornithologist, her protagonist and alter ego. She called him "Bird" and made him her narrator. After a period of writer's block, she decided to call forth Bird in a dream, hoping he would tell her what came next in the story. A huge version of Bird appeared in her sleep that night. He pantomimed the turning of a key and said, "Unlock the door. All I have to do is pick up the pencil and write." Nancy didn't know what to make of this. It didn't help her get going again. So we went to stay at a friend's cottage, hoping the vacation would give us fresh inspiration. The cottage was cold. We tucked ourselves in bed to read by the light of the white gas lantern. The rest of this story can be told better by Nancy, who published an essay about it in the *Utne Reader:*

With the lantern still burning, we quickly fell into a deep sleep. Soon a hazy image of the human-sized Bird appeared in my dream. He tried desperately to tell me something but couldn't reach me with his voice. Just when I began to feel as if I was being sucked into a region way beneath the realm of dreams, I vaguely heard Bird say, "I can't lift my head off the pillow." My immediate impulse was to try and lift my own head. I couldn't. In a panic, I struggled to wake myself but my body remained submerged. A battle took place between my will and my physical self as I tried to move my hand toward Pierre. It seemed forever before he stirred awake enough to share the realization that something was drastically wrong with both of us. With great effort we managed to roll our bodies to the edges of the bed and drop onto the floor. Surprisingly I felt no pain as I struck. Gasping for air we crawled toward the door dragging our bodies like huge, heavy carcasses behind us. After a long struggle I reached the door but couldn't coordinate my muscles to lift my arm. When Pierre actually grasped the doorknob, he didn't have the strength to turn it. Knowing it was our last chance for survival, Pierre grabbed the doorknob again and swung the door open. A gust of fresh air caressed our faces. Out on the patio we lay spread-eagled, breathing deeply the air that smelled sweeter than any air anywhere. We realized later that because we had kept all the windows closed the lantern had consumed the oxygen. If I had died that night, my book would never have been completed. Because Bird was in the process of being created within my imagination, my life meant his life. I discovered that the creatures we give life to are as determined as we are to stay alive until they have lived out their story. Not only do they live for us but at times we live for them.

Pure Lies

The best high school within reachable distance of San Miguel was in Celaya, forty miles away. It was run by the Catholic order of Marista Brothers. Our daughter Carla wanted to study there, so I took her to visit the director. He was a stiff martinet who wore a tightly cinched tie and a wool suit in the heat of August. He bade us have a seat in front of his desk, then went to sit behind it under a reproduction of *The Last Supper*. He started off asking questions about Carla's background, affecting the language of a professional pedant. But he relaxed into good humor when he learned that I had spent my childhood in France not far from the teacher-training school for the entire world order of Maristas. We switched to speaking French. He loved that. Everything seemed to be going well and I was feeling sure that Carla was about to be accepted into the school when the director asked what I did for a living. I told him I wrote books, thinking he'd be impressed. But I saw a look of suspicion bordering on panic. He switched back to Spanish to ask what kind of books I wrote. *"Novelas,"* I said. He leaned back, horrified. *"Novelas?"* He waved his hand in front of his face as if to ward off an evil apparition. I could see him trying to remember the Marista party line. *"Novelas,"* he pronounced with outrage. *"Puras mentiras."* (Pure lies.) He rang his buzzer, told his secretary to bring in the next applicant, and dismissed us without so much as an *adiós.* God, was I pissed off. I figured this man must have been raised in the same nineteenth-century tradition that got Madame Bovary into such trouble for reading novels. Night after night, I had fantasies of encountering the director in a bar, in a store, on a bus. It was always the same. I would give him a piece of my mind and then punch him in the snoot. During periods of frustration when I had fallen over my typewriter long after midnight, pounding my head into my crossed arms, I rehearsed versions of what I would shout in his face. "Don't you realize what the novelist's art is all about! It's about truth! Pure lies? You think it's as easy as that? Facts are easy. Fiction wants your blood! I wasted two years and a thousand pages writing the facts about my first wife's death. But it wouldn't do. What looked like truth was either too self-debasing or too self-serving. I'm having to write fiction so I can arrive at some kind of detachment. I'm killing myself writing this novel. And you're telling me it's pure lies! Asshole!" As often as I gave that "brother" a piece of my mind and then finished off the fantasy by ever more insanely beating the shit out of him, I never did see him again. If I did now, I would rush to embrace him. I'd thank him for giving me the perseverance not to give up on my novel, and not to compromise the moment of truth when I found it, even though I knew the novel would sell better had I provided an escape into illusion.

Ginsberg's Blessing
Keeps Me Grounded

I found Allen Ginsberg holed up in a pad above Ferlinghetti's publication office. He greeted me from a messy floor mattress, endearingly paunchy in his sleeveless undershirt, a man at home in his own skin. For all his latter-day Buddhist ways, Ginsberg had always seemed to me to be the rabbi of our bohemian generation, a combination of Old Testament prophet and psalmist. I was grateful to him for liberating poetry from the priests of the academy and restoring it to a prophetic role, back on the streets in the spirit of Whitman. Allen was putting together a book on the death of Cassady, and I had arrived after a long bus trip to report. I stepped gingerly amidst the correspondence and snapshots so characteristically strewn all over the floor, and thought to myself how hard he had worked to actualize the vision of his friends – Kerouac, Burroughs, Corso, Bowles, and the others – in the public eye. In writing and in photography, friendship was Ginsberg's greatest gift to the beat generation; he was a tireless publicist. What Ginsberg put across was this: that the story of the friends we've hung out with, whatever their importance to others, must be made precious to us if we are to take possession of our myth. It is with our friends in our most ordinary moments that we turn our destiny into what Kerouac called "sacred dust." Such moments can become our sacraments; the marks of suffering on our faces, life's validation. Anything that makes us forsake complete presence in the here-and-now only distracts us from what matters most, which is that we are daily blessed by the most mundane doings of our tribe, our pals. Call them crooks, saints, somebodies or nobodies, it doesn't matter. We love the story of our life because of them. All of us in the North Beach bohemian world had come to love our lives more because of the myth Ginsberg had created about us. True, some wanted to escape from that myth. I had decided not to tell Ginsberg how Cassady complained at the end about being stuck in the beat-hero role. And I remembered how Ferlinghetti once sent me to Bixby Creek to keep watch on a cabin where he'd installed Kerouac, fearing that Jack would break his promise and sneak off again somewhere to self-destruct before he'd finished another book. By the time Ginsberg was walking me down the stairs, I knew I'd have to run if I wanted to catch my plane. But Allen was now belly-to-belly with me on the sidewalk, hands pressed together while he intoned the Diamond Sutra. This sutra is very long and it smelled of Ginsberg's lunch. Twenty minutes passed while I struggled between the desire to be entirely attentive to what seemed an interminable blessing, and the desire to sprint away in hopes of still catching that very important and expensive flight to a job interview. By the time Ginsberg bowed, I knew the plane had been missed. But, lying in my sleeping bag that night, I felt a great sense of relief. I had to admit to myself that, for the sake of a more secure future, one can be too eager to rush toward a job one doesn't really want. As far as I was concerned, that was the message of the Diamond Sutra.

A Leaky Cucumber

One of the reasons Nancy and I rented the house on Lake Carnelian outside of Stillwater, Minnesota, is that it was two miles down the end of a long dirt road through a beautiful pine forest. I had visions of taking daily walks up that road to the highway and back. But this turned out to be too perilous because of two huge Great Danes. When they heard me coming, they would spring out onto the road, plant themselves at its center, and start barking menacingly in their powerful baritone voices until I turned back. The neighbors told me these dogs were named Hulk and Hurt. Nobody dared cross their path; complaints to the police about them had gone unheeded. We would be smart not to let them get close unless we were in the car—with our windows rolled up, by the way, because when they attacked a car they went right for the face in the window. This really frosted me. Much as I loved dogs, fear of the menacing ones had been implanted in my system by the rabid dog that had attacked me when I was an infant (the

159

consequent shots in my stomach didn't help things). Because of this fear, I found myself stuck with not being able to take my yearned-for walks. One morning, I decided I'd had enough. The road was public property, dammit. I gathered my courage and set forth. Breathing evenly, keeping a regular stride, I tried to stay calm, though it would have been impossible not to anticipate the time when the dogs were going to spring out and set up their roadblock. It didn't happen. As I passed their house, all was silent. I strode onward, keeping my eyes straight forward until . . . lo! I was beyond the danger point. I continued my walk feeling liberated, delighting now in the beauty and fragrance of the pine forest. Then a bursting forth from behind a bush and they were on me side by side. Barking for all they were worth, their horrifying faces – red-eyed, slavering, right up there a few inches from mine – backed me up against a tree. To my amazement, I was able to stay calm. In a steady voice I said, "Nice Hurt. Nice Hulk. Good Dogs. Go home now." This only fueled their rage. I could see that if I didn't somehow walk away, it was only a matter of time before they got on with the business of tearing my face off. I shouted a commanding "Stay!", stepped forth from the tree, and walked right between them, feeling the heat of their nostrils being blown into my ears. They followed me home, sniffing and snarling at the back of my neck. When I entered the house, I stood in front of Nancy and spread out my arms, amazed at myself, damn proud of what I'd just done. "I actually mastered my fear," I declared. "It's a good thing too, because if they had smelled the slightest fear on me, that would have been it. I'd have been dead meat. But you should have seen me, Nan. I was calm as a cucumber." She pointed to my crotch. "Tell me then," she said, "What's that big wet spot doing on the front of your pants?"

How I Saved the Life
of the Father I Killed

After I'd dragged my father from the car and laid him on the ground next to the tennis court where he and I had played the fatal set, I'd run to the nearest house to call an ambulance, asking the intern on the phone what I could do to try and revive him. He'd given me quick instructions on CPR. Running back, I'd found Ginette and my brother in a panic. I'd straddled my father and struck him on the chest, breathed into his mouth. Nothing had worked. Ginette had wailed that I should never have allowed him to play such a long set. "You knew he was having trouble with his heart." "I didn't," I said. "Nobody told me." "You killed him!" she'd screamed. The words had put a wound in my own heart that would not heal. I had a recurrent fantasy that lasted seventeen years: I saw myself there beside the Hope Ranch tennis courts in Santa Barbara bringing my father back to life. Then one day I walked into a bank in Stillwater, Minnesota, to meet my wife, who had gone in to set up a checking account. I thought a stickup was going on.

The customers and tellers seemed frozen in fear, all facing in the direction of the vault, including my wife and the woman at a table interviewing her. "Pierre," Nancy cried, "there's a man in there dying. Go save him." Running to the vault, I found the young bank manager wringing his hands beside a body on the floor—a big farmer in overalls lying on his back, white-faced, mouth open. "He's dead," the young man said, "No breath. No pulse. We've called the ambulance." I got down and straddled the farmer. Everything I'd fantasized doing to my father, I did to him. For what seemed a long time he didn't respond. Then, with one hard shove at the base of his ribs, I heard that most miraculous of all sounds: the breath of new life. I'd heard it a few weeks earlier while assisting at the birth of my first grandchild. That high first cry of an infant was exhilarating; but this deep, hoarse, sucking sound was no less so. Twice the farmer quit on me, and twice I got him to breathing again. When the medics arrived, they said the man wouldn't have made it without me. I left the bank feeling that a heavy debt had finally been paid; and my heart wound healed. A few days later, a woman called to say that many people depended on her father; she wanted me to know how grateful they all were that I had saved his life. I said, "I didn't just save *your* father's life. I saved *my* father's life. I'm as grateful as you are."

Cut the Duck!

Nancy was in love with a Peking duck she named Lunker. To judge from the state of his corkscrew "noodle" when she held him, he was in love with her too. I was jealous. He had taken over the house. He'd rush at me and nip at my ankle when I hugged her; he took over the upstairs tub for long afternoon splashes with his beloved. He finally became so obnoxious with our guests that Nancy agreed to take him to an estate in the country where there were creatures of his own species to play with. But he got in so many fights that he was confined with the chickens to a coop. We found him all muddy when we came to visit, the chickens rushing at him to pluck out his tail feathers. He went crazy with joy when Nancy rescued him. He gave his happy cry all the way home. Then the landlady paid a visit. "You said he was a chicken," she snapped. "He's no chicken. Get rid of him." So we took him to another farm where he resigned himself to an arranged marriage, had a few kids, but then died . . . from missing his true love, I must regretfully admit. After his death, Nancy and I conceived a show of songs, stories, and dances about the values of the small family farm. We took our show to some thirty small farm towns in Minnesota on the local Chautauqua Circuit, performing at town halls, churches, libraries. Thousands of family farms were having to be sold; farmers were committing suicide; Main Street businesses were closing down. Because our songs reminded the farmers of the kind of intimacy with the land and animals many had sacrificed for fencepost-to-fencepost profit making, we caused a lot of tears; and seeing how the government had conned farmers into expanding beyond their means, then having to sell out to the corporate owners, we became more radicalized. Nancy had a stuffed white puppet duck who looked a lot like Lunker. For comic relief, she told stories about him. Children always rushed up to pet him. When we appeared at a big event on the state capitol grounds called A Taste of Minnesota, we sang about the greed of the president, the corporations, the bankers. A rock band was blasting away across the lawn from us. Standing at different mikes, Nancy and I couldn't hear each other. After one of our shows, the woman in charge of the Chautauqua marched up to remind us that our show was being sponsored by a corporation (the public library association), we relied on certain banks for private funding, and we had no right to insult President Reagan. "Cut all the left-wing stuff," she said, "and since you can't seem to sing in harmony, cut the duets." We couldn't believe it. That would take just about everything out of our show. But then came the final insult. As she was walking away, our supervisor looked back over her shoulder. Glaring at Nancy, she shouted, "And cut the duck!" We burst into laughter, walked off the stage and rolled with Lunker in the grass. Cut our dear Lunker? No, no, no, we promised. We would never do that.

Ghosts
of Our Aborted Children

I was driving my mother and my aunt to Wisconsin. My aunt got to talking about how much she and my uncle had envied my mother for having "two such fine boys" – not having children had caused her and my uncle such sorrow. I told about how happy I'd been when my first child turned out to be a girl. Not having a sister, I'd always wished I knew more about what girls were like growing up. I still wished so much I had a sister. My mother burst into tears. The sobbing went on and on. Finally I pulled over to the side of the road. There at the way-side rest Mom told how Dad drove her downtown one day, up an alley, left her in front of an abortion mill, said she either went through with the abortion he'd schedule for her, or he was leaving her – and then drove off to teach class. It was a horribly bloody, painful experience having the little girl killed and torn out of her. She barely made it home on the streetcar. Dad didn't come home until late. Mom had never been able to forgive him for this. Never had she stopped grieving the death of her daughter. I, who had supported (and still do) a woman's right freely to choose abortion, was stunned. So that is what her frequent tears were all about. Ever since then, I have wondered about my sister. As the years go by, the memory of her lives more and more in me, as if I'd known her. I see her in my mind's eye. I imagine her moving about among us, a very happy, singing spirit, not unlike my daughter Michele. This aborted sister of mine seems to become more of a presence for me as I grow older, almost as if she's becoming whole, manifesting her realized presence in preparation for the day when we finally meet. Ten years ago, a young woman I'd had a brief affair with came calling. I was now happily married, with two newly adopted children. The young woman and I took a walk. She became very solemn as she told the wretched story of how she'd almost bled to death aborting my child. My psyche was split in two when I heard this. The part of me I inherited from my father was relieved because I knew I would have opposed an abortion had she told me she was pregnant, so I would have had an unwanted child to raise in some kind of complicated relationship with a woman I was much too old for, and not in love with in a marrying way. The part inherited from my mother grieved, and grieves still, and wonders about this child too. What would he or she have been like? A few times, driving alone, the child's ghost has been like a presence sitting in the seat beside me, chatting happily, laughing with me. I wonder how many of us have these ghosts or spirits of aborted children lingering at the edges of our consciousness. Perhaps we keep them alive to assuage our personal and communal guilt or remorse. Perhaps we simply love them and can't let them go. They are certainly the most privately thought about creatures ever to live inside the ocean of our flesh.

Ra's Cave

The most beautiful work of art I ever saw conceived and created by a single person was called "the heart chamber" by the artist. Everyone else called it Ra's cave. Ra didn't name himself after the Egyptian god. He was named by a nephew who couldn't pronounce Robert. Ra is the least pretentious of persons – a wiry, hard-muscled, good-natured, though socially shy man, originally from New York, now off in Colorado building a series of shrines. Before he left, he buried his cave, covered it with earth, and went to great pains to hide the trail. Too many people had been making pilgrimages to the cave as word kept spreading all over the world. Christians, Buddhists, Hindus, spiritual visionaries of all persuasions had made tiny shrines for themselves in the cave's niches. They came there to meditate, chant, pray. The cave was on public lands, and Ra was afraid he had unwittingly created a cause for ecological damage. Not that anybody left litter behind. Only once was the cave vandalized. There were no grafitti. But a few trees had been chopped down and used for firewood by people who camped near the cave. That was enough to make Ra spend a year hauling earth back to his cave to bury it. It took him some four years of pretty much constant work to carve it out of a sandstone cliff high on a ridge an hour's drive from Santa Fe, another two-mile uphill hike from his adobe hut on the Rio Grande. He was in such great shape that he would run all the way up every day to leave water for the guests and seed for the birds. You couldn't see the cave until you were right in front of the little door with the birds flitting at the nearby feeder. After you crawled inside, you stood up and found yourself in an awesomely beautiful white chamber with carved pillars, platforms, meditation seats, and side chambers you could climb up into so as to look out through oval windows on the spectacular views of the Sangre de Cristo Mountains, the red adobe cliffs – ancient pueblo cliff-dwelling territory – and the river gorge. Jewels, candles, shells, pods, and images of avatars adorned the niches. The circular seats and sensuously shaped walls, chambers and columns of the cave reminded me of the late découpage carvings of Matisse, but in three dimensions. In that cave, you stood or sat inside a sacred sculpture. The first time I hiked there, three Tibetan monks joined me in chanting. The resonance made my hair stand up. There was a kiva fireplace for those who spent the night. A desk for people who wanted to sit and write in the guest book. The remarks were variations of thanksgiving for the cave's magic. We understood Ra's reasons for burying it; but some of us suffered anguish, even re-sentment. We felt he didn't have the right to take the cave from us. Ra said he was sorry, but he hoped people would find the cave now inside the chamber of their own hearts.

Get off My Grass

My friend John Muir had been writing science fiction books for fifteen years without selling a one. Then he met his wise new partner, Eve. She said, in effect, "John, what you are is a mystical mechanic. Earth is your element. Bring your writing down from space." She encouraged him to take a VW bug entirely apart, lay the parts on the ground, write instructions on how to put the car back together again. Eve would go out on the plaza and bring home the three most idiotic people she could find. She would read them a line of the instructions. If all could follow, fine; if not, John rewrote. Many people, he discovered, are too ashamed to admit they don't understand professional repair manuals. If the instructions say, "Pick up the wrench and unscrew the nut," the idiot might say, "What's a wrench?" John explained everything, even saying when the work should be abandoned for a little relaxation, like going into the house and "balling the old lady." Nobody would publish his *Compleat Idiot's Guide to VW Re-*

pair, so he set up his own press, JMP, published it himself, and made a fortune. He built a large house in San Miguel for his maid and all her children and relatives, then built a small house behind it for himself and Eve. A community of friends would gather there for hot-pool parties and the strategy sessions for New Age projects John and Eve financed and encouraged. Every year they hosted a beach party attended by a crowd of "family." John smoked Prince Albert pipe tobacco rolled into cigarettes. He also had his daily joint and extolled the virtues of grass. After moving his press to Santa Fe, he got lung cancer. Ironically, it moved to the brain as he worked on a book about how to think. His theory was that most people don't know how to "take things in flat." As soon as a subject comes up, their reflex is to reach into the mind's filing cabinet so as to ready themselves with a preconceived remark. He, who had worked on space projects for NASA, believed that every new situation should be examined with unworn wheels of thought, not with retreads. As he was dying, the family gathered in Santa Fe. He had a hard time letting go. Finally, Eve said, "John, people are tired of waiting, they have other things to do, get on with it." So he did. I had to miss that occasion. But fifteen years later my friend Marty invited me to see the house he'd bought in Santa Fe. He said, "There's some guy named Muir buried in the back yard." The grave was a beautiful rectangle of grass with fruit trees and herbal shrubs over each *chakra.* At the sex *chakra* was an upstanding boulder. I asked to be left alone, stepped onto the grave, and knelt down with my back to this boulder. "John," I said, "I don't know whether there's such a thing as channeling. But if there is, you can use me to dictate the rest of your book." I was startled to hear his voice speak loud and clear: "Pierre, dammit, would you please get off my grass."

My Mother Sees

Living as I do now in an area where our Hispanic and Indian neighbors revere their elders and keep them crucially involved with the family, I have come to feel remorse for the way I allowed my mother to go on living alone for so many years in her little house in Norman, Oklahoma, to which my dad had abandoned her after divorcing her to marry the woman he loved. He prospered but never sent her a cent beyond a pitiful settlement; the bank where she had worked for twenty-six years collapsed, failing to pay off on its profit-sharing plan; the inheritance her brother left her was mostly ripped off by the executor. Her friends died one by one, mostly in solitude. So many rapes and other crimes against old ladies had occurred in the town where she had loved to walk, stopping on the sidewalk to chat, that she stayed bolted in after dark. Her car had to be given up after she drove to a school and went looking for the classroom where she imagined she was teaching, then had a wreck on the way home. Her neighbors called to warn that she'd been deceiving us; she really couldn't take care of herself anymore. My brother and sister-in-law found her a good nursing home in Minneapolis. My job was to go help her get packed and to the airport. The way she lingered over each thing broke my heart. She could hardly let go of anything – not because she would need it in her small room, but because every item of clothing, jewelry, furniture was attached to a memory that brought tears to her eyes. We packed it all and sent it to be stored in my brother's garage. That last week I was with her, I saw how she had struggled with incontinence; I learned from her neighbors how she had taken many falls, sometimes being found in the snow or mud of the yard sitting there for hours, unable to get up, an apologetic smile on her face when someone finally came to her rescue. When her friends became few, she took to talking to her tree, to the artificial birds that filled her house, to the real birds and squirrels. The tree in the front yard had become her father. The scar in the backyard maple was the face of my first wife. When it was time to go, I suggested she say a last good-bye to the trees, but she wouldn't. She hobbled straight to the car without looking back. At the airport I left her, a hunchbacked, smiling little gnome. That night I sat in her house, in the recliner chair she'd left in front of an old black-and-white TV. I watched Johnny as she had night after night. She had depended on his support much more than on mine. My sorrow and shame were immense. A few months later, the last time I phoned, she said she couldn't talk now; she was watching Pavaroti on TV. She was found dead the next night in front of the new TV, in her maple rocking chair; behind her, a painting of winter in the village I lived in. I'd told her, when she said she'd like to come live with us: "Gosh, Mom, don't we wish. But winters here are just too cold." She'd said, "I see."

Good God

One of my students in a class for the learning-disabled was Herman, a man with ardent eyes in a head so huge he seemed sometimes to have to lean it on my shoulder to keep it from falling over as we sat side by side struggling over the problem of how to release him from his longtime imprisonment inside the world of those who can't read. Herman was a fine diesel mechanic, but he couldn't advance because he couldn't read instructions in the repair manuals. During his childhood, a teacher had so terrorized him that he'd run away from school. The trauma had shut something off in his brain so that he couldn't make the connection between vowels and the sounds they made. For some reason, he had no trouble with consonants. When we started together, he had already been working in the language lab for two years. Herman was so embarrassed by his difficulties that he made matters worse by attempting to read consonant-vowel combinations only in a murmured voice. Day after day we tried, and day after day "Mi" would come out a murmured "M," "Ka" a "K," etc. On the last day of the term, I decided I had to go back to the beginning, to the very first day of biblical creation. I said, "Herman, what are these two letters?" Spacing them wide apart, I wrote down *g* and *d.* He said, "G...D...Gd!" I wrote two *o*'s between the letters and said, "Good, Herman just like this word says. But watch. I erase one of the *o*'s, and what do I have? A brand-new word with a different sound, because now there's only one *o*, and it sounds like 'ah.' So: try reading this word now." "Gd!" he blurted. "Herman," I said, "I want you to stand up and shout out this word I've written, vowel and all. Howl it, scream it, I don't care, but give it all your might. I stood. Dutifully he got up and stood beside me. He looked sheepishly about. Other students were working at the computers. I held up the page with the word *God* on it. He began to sputter. "G...D..." "Loud!" I said. His lips exploded a "Gd!" Desperately, he tried again, louder this time: "G! D! Gd! Gd!" The other students looked up from their computers. I said, "Show them you can do this, Herman. Shout it out." His stomach puffed up, his shoulders rose; air filled his lungs. I shook the sheet of paper in front of his eyes. He stared at it frantically, drew his head back, cried out, "G...G...GAAAAAAAAAAAAAAAAAAAAAAAAAAAAAAAAAAAHD!" The students burst into applause. Herman's eyes were wild. His mouth was open wide; he wouldn't let go of the sound. On and on it went until it vanished inside the very heart of creation. Never in my life had a word sounded so beautiful. I was in tears. With the vowel-barrier broken, Herman went on to become a passable reader, good enough to make it through the composition courses. He's going to get his degree in diesel mechanics soon.

I Am Given the Dalai Lama's
Blessing at Last

Long before I saw and heard the Dalai Lama and knew he was the humorous and very human peacemaker I had imagined, the mystery of his life in all its incarnations stirred my spiritual imagination. I built stories around him combining what I knew of Tibetan Buddhism with my own experiences in the United States. When the British Penguin edition of my tales about him came out, I lost my only copy, sent for another, and was told there were no more. How could it have vanished so fast? The answer came during a scene at the post office when an angry woman slapped a magazine from the Himalayan Institute on the counter, glowered at me, and left. She had marked an article by an Englishman who was one of the first to enter Tibet trekking from Nepal. He said the Chinese guards at the Potala were handing out "a hostile book on the Dalai Lama by Pierre Delattre." Of course, I was deeply hurt, for I was not hostile to the Dalai Lama, but an advocate who loved him. I wondered for years whether the Dalai Lama had read my book; if so, whether he enjoyed it or felt offended. I fantasized giving him the book, then holding his hands, looking into his eyes, and receiving his blessing. When he visited Santa Fe, I couldn't get close to him, so I gave the book to a member of his entourage, who promised to give it to him. The secretary at the inn where he was staying mailed me the book with a note saying it had been found "on the highway." This hurt me for months until a man named Bob Shaw called to say he'd just read my book and thought the Dalai Lama would love it. Shaw had been the Dalai Lama's official photographer in Santa Fe. He said he knew how he could get the book to him at his home in India. He said the Dalai Lama had been showered with so many gifts during his American tour that gifts had been left lying around everywhere. Sometimes the limousine was so filled with gifts that his small staff couldn't think of what to do except set them alongside the road so the Dalai Lama could get back in after having stepped out to bless people. What a relief. Bob turned out to be my spiritual twin. He had also been raised in Oklahoma, attended the University of Chicago Divinity School, had been ordained without ever planning to enter the ministry, had become a more widely ranging seeker, demitted, gone to Mexico just like me, worked under the influence of Ivan Ilyich, published in the same magazines, on and on the same until we both landed in New Mexico as visual artists. I told Bob how I regretted not receiving the Dalai Lama's blessing. Bob said, "All of us were feeling slighted because we weren't allowed to get close to him. But just as he was about to board his plane, I found myself reaching for him. Amidst all the flurry, he grasped my hands in his and stopped all motion for a long time. Smiling, he looked me directly in the eyes. Those warm, steady hands infused my whole body with a marvelous peacefulness. Now I can pass his blessing on to you." And so he has.

Posturing

The healer Martin Weiner came out for a visit. While we were taking a walk up the arroyo, he saw that I was limping and asked if I'd hurt myself. I said that my hip had been in a lot of pain again, ever since I'd started working on a lecture I had to give in front of a large audience. It was the same pain I'd undergone two years ago when I started teaching yoga to a group of neighborhood women. The day before the class started, I'd checked over some postures in my yoga book and discovered to my consternation that I had been crossing my legs wrong ever since I'd begun doing the lotus posture some fifteen years before. Instead of crossing the left leg over the right, I should have been crossing the right over the left. Not that it probably mattered, but I decided I better do it correctly in front of my students or they might check it out and think I didn't know what I was doing. My legs were so used to crossing the other way that when I had to force them hard into the different posture (with the women watching, my pride wouldn't allow me

177

to admit that I couldn't do it comfortably), I yanked my leg hard sideways and twisted something out of joint, maybe tore a ligament. The pain hadn't bothered me for about a year, but now it was back, though I wasn't even sitting in the lotus anymore. Weiner listened to all this, then asked, "What posture are you forcing yourself into now?" I thought it over. "Funny you should ask," I said. "Just before you arrived, I was writing to my brother telling him that I couldn't decide what kind of posture to take for the lecture. Should I assume an academic stance, reading from a prepared manuscript, or should I take a more casual posture and speak chattily from notes." Marty pressed the flat of his hand hard on my hip and said, "You don't have to take postures anymore, Pierre. Just say what you have to say." Immediately the pain drained out of my hip. My attitude, not only toward lecturing but toward writing, changed. I began to feel much more healthy and contented in my work.

Starting from
Where You're Standing

The adobe house we live in up an arroyo near a village of artist/farmers is on the edge of Bureau of Land Management land. We can hike from my back door into the red-earth country of the Sangre de Cristo foothills, through piñon and juniper stands, up over buttes, escarpments, and mesas, never meeting another human being, only an occasional coyote, mountain lion, rabbit, or rattlesnake. Much of the book you are reading was written while I was seated in a cave I discovered, carved out of the cliff by an ancient hunter. His chipping stones are still here by my side; the petroglyph he carved of a snake is on the wall behind my head; the coals of his firepit in front of my crossed legs. I'm looking down at a copse of cottonwoods, cattails, and reeds where the animals come to drink. I am in bliss here. My wife back at the house is painting her interior landscapes. Four years ago, it looked like we'd have to leave this place we love so much. We were broke. My last book hadn't sold. The galleries weren't interested in Nancy's paintings. It's hard to find work in this territory. What to do? We were standing in the arroyo – a dry wash that briefly turns into a river after the rains – wondering how we could possibly come up with the money to survive here. Then we remembered a neighbor couple telling us that they'd been in the same predicament seven years before – broke, longing to stay in our village. They remembered what a wise woman had told them: If you don't know how to make a living, pay closer attention to where you are right now. Then start from where you're standing. My friends happened to be standing in front of a grove of willows. They began making the willow twig screens that you will see in many of the fine homes of New Mexico. Their business is thriving. I looked around me. What I saw were rocks. At my feet lay an oval rock about the size of my head. I picked it up and lugged it home. Finding an image in the rock's veins and ridges, I got out my acrylic paints and set to work. Alvaro and Barbara, my Happiness Gorilla friends, had moved to Truchas, a village up in the mountains, and had just finished building their art gallery. They chanced to drop by that day, saw the rock, took it up to their gallery and sold it. Since then, my paintings on rock have not only sold well, but searching for them and carrying them home has increased my happiness and kept me in excellent shape. Taking them up to the gallery is always a great excuse for a visit with the Happiness Gorillas. Searching for images in the rocks has increased my kinship with the earth and has grounded my soul in the mysticism of my own name. When Nancy looked about, that day up the arroyo, she saw the wildflowers and grasses. For two years, she turned these into wreathes she sold at the fairs. Daily intimacy with natural colors transformed her palette so beautifully that she has become a very successful painter, showing at galleries in Santa Fe and Boulder.

Are Spaceships
Living Creatures?

Given half a chance to believe in the marvelous, I take it, and I have found that my beliefs end up being – let us say – "verified" by the scientific community just as often as the play-it-safe disbelief of the sceptics is relegated to the arcane. A case in point is the UFO. Sunning on the roof of chapel-house, my first wife Lois and I watched a fleet of seven move slowly across our line of vision a half minute apart, through a windless blue sky, right over the stadium where the first cyclotron had been built by Fermi and company. They were cigar shaped, just as you read in the books by fanatics, with bands of bluish green light along the edges and what seemed like yellow-glowing portholes. They were as clear to our sight as any solid object I lift and pass in front of my eyes. Over Lake Michigan, they hovered, then shot at an angle out of sight. We learned to keep our mouths shut, but wondered how others could have missed them. Then I read about Admiral Perry's steam-driven ships entering a bay in Japan. Nobody reported seeing them for quite some time, though numerous strollers were passing on the beach and boats were anchored nearby. Credulity has its rewards. Later, four of us were followed at night on a Mexican country road by a fiery light, blue-green at the center. We stopped, grew frightened. The panic of our screaming (we decided) caused the ship to vanish before our eyes. My theory is that space ships are seen when they slow down to the speed of light, fiery at first, glowing, and then quite like any airplane to our vision. They are able instantly to reenter a dimension faster-than-light. Swimming off Garafon reef at Isla de Mujeres, I was watching fish with phosphorescent spots move past when it dawned on me that what I might have seen were not vehicles at all, but living creatures who feed on light, and flit from star to star as fish flit from rock to rock. My third sighting was at Chaco Canyon, three a.m., the same glowing ball of blue-green light. Six of us saw it manifest in midair right over a kiva, silent and peaceful like the others. It remained suspended there for about fifteen seconds, then also vanished. The hope of seeing another is so strong that it has affected my dream life. In one dream, seven beautiful women in long hooded cloaks were standing at a distance from the house in the moonlight. I invited them in. They drank the tea I served, gazed silently into the fire, then got up, looked at Nancy's paintings, and left. It occurred to me the next morning while doing yoga that the number seven, so often reported in sightings both of "saucers" and of portholes on mother ships, might be related in some way to the *chakras*. Certain caterpillars in Brazil hump along until they reach a feeding spot, break into segments, browse, and return to become a single body. Who knows yet how UFOs break up and reassemble, manifest, and unmanifest in our space/time?

Faith in Memory

Some people believe that memory is largely invented. I don't. It used to embarrass me that I saw my life as such a series of wonderful episodes. A friend accused me of making things up so that my life would seem more exciting than others'. I argued that all our lives are miraculous if only we're willing to view them that way. But I found myself downplaying or denying the more miraculous events, wondering whether I wasn't making things up. After all, I'm a fiction writer. Yet the world kept on pulsing new amazements, providing a constant series of epiphanies, illuminations, peak experiences. I know that if – out of inattention or cynicism or a moribund view of the world – we don't respond to the wondrous, then we get what we expect: a confirmation that life is unsurprising. I remember precisely when I gave up doubting my memories once and for all. There was a story I liked to tell about the first school I attended. It was at the top of a hill in the southern French village of Privas. Across the schoolyard was a jail. The prisoners used to watch us through their barred windows during our recess. They thrust their arms through the bars, begging us to throw them a piece of fruit from our lunch boxes. Among the boys, generosity on this score was a matter of honor, and throwing accurately enough for the prisoner to catch was a matter of pride. The prison was three stories high. Us little boys only had the strength to throw to the disturbers of the peace on the first floor. Only once did I manage to fling a banana all the way to one of the petty criminals on the second floor. I envied the big boys who could throw to the hardened criminals at the very top. My hero was a big boy who brought a bag lunch to school, but disdained eating more than a few bites before he flung the bag way up to a man with piteous eyes and a plaintive voice, whom we'd been warned was a murderer. I wished I could throw high and far enough to establish such a bond with someone so forlorn. I used to tell my wife, Nancy, about this dream of sharing my lunch with a murderer, but secretly I had begun to suspect myself. Had I made up this whole story about the jail? Nancy said, "Let's find out. Let's go to France." So we did. Privas was now a smoggy city. Yet we managed to find my grandfather's former church in the old section – a tinier building than I remembered, of course. From there, Nancy had me close my eyes. She walked me up the hill. When we got to the top, she had me look. There stood my old school, now a music conservatory. "As for your jail . . ." Nancy said, and smiled with what I thought was mockery. I turned with a shrug, ready to admit that my jail was pure invention. But there it was. A ruin now, but otherwise the same. I wanted to get down on my knees and give thanks. Those barred windows quite suddenly had restored once and for all a faith in my own memory. Such faith, I realized, frees us to an unbounded faith in the creation itself.

Love on a Winter's Night

When I had written down the last of the "episodes" in this book, I went up to bed feeling very contented. It was such a bitter cold winter night, with the full moon just surfacing over the bluff outside our window, that I kept on my beret and my long johns. Tucked up against Nancy, I knew I wouldn't sleep. The full moon always kept me awake. But that was okay. It gave me more time to savor the love for the woman I held in my arms. She was having one of her moaning dreams, the kind where I felt she might be falling too deeply into somewhere; and so I held her tight, to let her body know that the bed at least was still horizontal, and all was safe. I tried to remember the stories I'd written down over the last year or so. I pondered their mystery and their meaning yet again and wondered whether anyone would ever read them and, if so, what effect they would have on minds and emotions. Then I let them go. I imagined readers out there under this same moon; and I hoped my book would nudge them toward writing down some episodes from their own lives, so that their friends and family at least would possess a little book to know them by. I realized that of all the episodes in my life, the one that I most loved to remember was the one that was taking place right now, the one I hoped nobody on earth would ever be deprived of for very long: this recurrent moment more beautiful and poetic than any other event I think we can know. Holding the person we love through a long, wakeful night, listening to their breathing and sometimes to their dreaming. Loving them silently in the pure bliss of contact with their body. This episode is the one I most treasure, the one that will be hardest to let go of when it becomes time for the final episode on earth.

About the Author

Pierre Delattre lives in an adobe house far up an arroyo in the foothills of the Sangre de Cristo Mountains between Taos and Santa Fe. He's a writer, painter, and teacher. He is the author of two novels, *Walking on Air* and *Tales of a Dalai Lama,* as well as many stories and poems. He has taught writing at the Universities of Minnesota and Alabama and for many years taught writing and aesthetics at the Instituto Allende in Mexico. He has worked in theater, film, and television and on a number of industrial jobs.

After taking his graduate degree in religion and the arts at the University of Chicago Divinity School, he ran a coffeehouse ministry in San Francisco's North Beach during the beat era, hosted a television series, "Against the Stream," and was an editor of the magazine *Beatitude,* which published many of the early beat poems.

Delattre has always had a special interest in the moral and spiritual aspects of emergent culture. He has been a teacher of yoga and of courses relating the arts to spiritual disciplines.

He is currently exhibiting his visual art at the Art Ventures Gallery in Santa Fe and his rock art at the Cardona-Hine Gallery in Truchas, New Mexico.

He serves as a contributing editor of *The Hungry Mind Review* and of *The* magazine.

This book was designed by Tree Swenson.

It is set in New Caledonia type by The Typeworks

and manufactured by Thomson-Shore on acid-free paper.

The cover painting is "Love on a Winter's Night,"

by Pierre Delattre.